Connecting the Dots

ROSS J. STONE

Bloomington, IN  Milton Keynes, UK

authorHOUSE™

AuthorHouse™
1663 Liberty Drive, Suite 200
Bloomington, IN 47403
www.authorhouse.com
Phone: 1-800-839-8640

AuthorHouse™ *UK Ltd.*
500 Avebury Boulevard
Central Milton Keynes, MK9 2BE
www.authorhouse.co.uk
Phone: 08001974150

First published by AuthorHouse 6/5/2006

ISBN: 1-4259-2916-8 (sc)

Printed in the United States of America
Bloomington, Indiana

This book is printed on acid-free paper.

BEFORE YOU START READING.......

this book, reading the back cover first will help the reader understand how and why this book was written. The contents following this page represent the thoughts sent to my business associates during the calendar year 2004. Thus, each Chapter represents a month of that year. No changes were or have been made from the original writings – they represent my thoughts when written, shaped by what I knew of the past, what was currently happening in the present, and what I divined for the future.

Again, whether you choose to 'see' things as expressed in the writings or in another manner is not important – the most important issue is that you find 'truths' that you can accept to define your financial world. A 'truth' that once was 'true' was expressed as "get a good education, get a good job, work hard and retire well in your Golden Years". Today, the term 'Golden Years' has lost the meaning it once held, and is not even uttered. This 'truth' of the past is no longer true today – nor will it ever be again.

Find your 'truths' – for the actions and decisions you make today will be based upon your 'truths' – and will thus define how you will live in the future.

Ross

Chapter One: January of 2004

Happy New Year to all of you!!! It is now 2004 - and in regards to the Book of the month, written by Alex Spanos - ' who is going to step through the door ?'

Thought I would review some of the headlines from the past several years, from 2001 through 2003 and compare them with what is happening today.

2001: Economic Expansion Ends - ten years of steady growth ceases with rising joblessness and sinking spirits (Sacto Bee, 11.01.01) The terrorist attack of 9.11 played a key role in pushing an already weak economy over the brink. People are losing their jobs.

2002: Fortune 500 has a new top dog - Wal-Mart will bump the lists tradition of manufacturer might (Sacto Bee, 01.24.02). Forty years after Sam Walton opened his first Wal-Mart, the 4,150 store global chain has overtaken Exxon Mobil as the largest company in the world. The most notable aspect is that a company that makes nothing would top a list long dominated by manufacturers. "It is indicative that we've made a big shift in this country to the service economy". (read that the Information Age).

Market recovery could be years away, experts say (Associated Press, Amy Baldwin, 04.13.02) Historically, economic recoveries have been forecast on Wall Street in a simple fashion: Stock prices rebound first and an earnings recovery occurs soon after. Gibbons Burke said: "Stocks are expensive right now. Companies either need to grow their earnings to justify the price, or prices have to come down."

Why You're Paying More - and Less – (Wall Street Journal, 11.03.02). "Those industries and businesses that are competing on a global market have no pricing power." They have to cut prices to remain competitive. Today, we have both wages and prices dropping - a deflationary action (deflation - widespread declines in wages and prices).

2003: Padded public pensions a ticking time bomb in budget crisis (Sacto Bee, 02.019.03). ...one small county, Mariposa, projects that when the new pension 'contributions' kick in next year, its costs will jump from $500,000 a year to $2.5 Million.

Now it's housing bubble that seems ready to pop (Sacto Bee, 03.09.03). Everyone now knows about the tech bubble because it has already burst; fewer recognize its near neighbor, the mortgage bubble, because they are living in it. Generations bought homes by borrowing 80% and paying it down over 30 years. No longer; the American home is just one more credit line to be tapped. As a percentage of personal income, mortgage debt has risen from 51% 25 years ago to over 100% today. In the last five (5!!!) years, mortgage debt has risen by 60%, or $2.2 Trillion. In 2001 and 2002, Americans extracted $300 Billion in cash from their homes via refi's and home equity loans. This infusion of cash is what has fueled rising consumer spending in the face of recession.

High on Tech (Sacto Bee, 04.13.03) "Ninety-eight percent of the innovation...is still in front of us (the Internet). "The mainstream thinks the game is over; the reality is it has not yet begun." Tony Perkins, the man who warned about the dot-com crash of 1999 in "The Internet Bubble".

CONNECTING THE DOTS:

There sure was a lotta 'dots' that came out over the past couple of years - and I think that each of you that have read the above information can connect your own 'dots'. We all know that the Information Age is moving ten times faster than the Industrial Age did, and that the next two or three years will witness massive changes in each of our lives. The question that is, and will not change, is: " How do you want to live during the coming years?" Your answer will provide your impetus in building your own business-model. The business model exists, the process is at the tip of our fingers and tongues. We have the system. Combined, these 'legs' of success can enable each of us to reach our goals and aspirations.

See you on the Hiways and the Biways!!!

KNOWLEDGE IS POWER;

IF NOT USED, IT IS ONLY INFORMATION

Ross

Chapter One: January 2004
Week Two

OK!!!

The New Year is fully upon us - and most everyone that Linda and I have talked with enjoyed the Holidays, and are really chomping at the bit to get up to full speed.

So, what headlines have we witnesses this past week?

1.   The median price home in the Sacramento area climbed to a whooooooping $367,000.00!!!

2.   Jobless rate fell to 5.7% during December.

3.   Wal-Mart is gathering a lot of attention: in the Sacramento Bee this past Friday, most of the Letters to the Editor were in regard to the effect that Wal-Mart is having on the American work force. (This was not an article – just a lot of letters from people out there in readership land)

CONNECTING THE DOTS:

1.   If you are like me, you must be wondering how people continue to afford to pay so much for a home! Now, just so we are all on the same page, the word median and average are NOT the same. An 'average' of a group of anything is the sum (total) of that group, divided by the number of things that were in that group. The 'median' of anything is just like the 'median' of a road - right in the middle. As the median of a road has approximately the same width on one side as the

other, the median of a group of numbers means there are the same number on one side as the other. So, saying the median price home climbed to $367,000 infers that there were the same number of homes that sold for less, as sold for more. Anyway - this is one heck of a HIGH median. Where do you think people are finding the money to pay the mortgage? Is it possible that people believe their job is not only safe, but that they will be receiving pay increases in the future? And how many jobs does it take to make that type of money?

2. The good news is that the jobless rate fell to 5.7% - but the bad news is that during December, while forecasters predicted the creation of some 150,000 new jobs, only 1,000 actually came into existence!!!!! This same news is what started to drive the DOW Jones down - investors are becoming more and more concerned with the question of: where are the jobs and what are the people doing that quit looking? Jobless people usually have less money to spend, which threatens any business. What is becoming known is that many people just QUIT looking for work - they got tired of not finding a decent paying job. Which leads me to item #3.

3. Boy oh boy - people are starting to become concerned with the power of Wal-Mart!!! As reported last year, W/M has more employees than the U.S. Army has soldiers!!! And W/M is the biggest gorilla out there - which frightens many manufacturers - since W/M has more and more power to control pricing/payment methods/etc. Now don't get me wrong, W/M is not doing anything illegal - just doing what they do better than almost anyone else has ever done it. And that scares a lot of people. Remember the 70,000 retail clerks down in So Cal that went on strike? They still are on strike, and from my view, have not only lost the battle, but the war as well. The issue of deflation has not disappeared - and will not. Wages remain stagnant; ROI continues to be either stagnant, or decreasing. The economic times that Leif Johnson

has referred to as being a driving force that fed his dramatic business growth in the past, he sees today. And he is correct. People are starting to become more and more concerned (that is politically correct speak for 'scared') about their own, and their families' financial future. If ever there was a time to get into gear and build your business, now is that time. You possess the answer for so many of the questions that your friends and family are asking.

Remember:

KNOWLEDGE IS POWER;
BUT IF NOT USED, JUST INFORMATION!

See Ya on the HiWays and BiWays.

Ross

Chapter One: January 2004
Week Three

Hi again to all of you!

This 'issue' of Money Talk will be a bit different from the normal format.

I would imagine that most, if not all, of you have seen the movie titled The Perfect Storm - or at least know that it is based upon a true occurrence. In a nutshell, a fishing boat found itself caught out at sea at the point of confluence of three big storms - creating what was to be called 'The Perfect Storm'. One that no one had ever seen before - or maybe had even occurred. So you can guess that this was one big, hairy, scary, terrible storm. What I now share is my vision of another 'Perfect Storm'.

It would appear that, economically speaking, there is another Perfect Storm brewing - the confluence of three major economic challenges that are afoot as I write.

The First storm has to do with the issue of Deflation. Wages continue to stagnate;worker unions seem to be more preoccupied with creating stronger health benefits than increasing wages. Jobs continue to disappear - in December it was reported that only 1,000 jobs were created in the entire United States! That is 20 jobs created per State (on average). Jobs continue to go overseas, manufacturing continues to move overseas, and wages in many cases seem to be going down (if one's wage does not go up each year, then by the nature of inflation, the wages really went down - weaker spending power). Prices, in many cases, are also going down - witness the power of Wal-Mart. Margins of profit are either frozen, or in decline.

The Second storm has to do with the issue of Pensions. As noted before, cumulatively - corporate pension plans are some $350 Billion in arrears of being fully funded. Congress is currently working on decreasing the amount that corporations must fund to - making the fund weaker, not stronger. Many of the same issues that pension plans are facing today are close to the same that the Savings and Loan industry faced back in 1989. In fact, '89 was an election year - just as this is an election year (Presidential in both!); the challenges were known - but not talked about - and definitely not addressed - until after the election year. The S & L mess cost the taxpayers of the U.S. in excess of $200 Billion. The branch of the U.S. Gov't that takes over pension plans of bankrupt companies had a $9 Billion surplus three years ago; today it is some $9 Billion in the HOLE! And the hole is getting larger. When the Gov't does take over the bankrupt pension plans, the beneficiaries do NOT receive the same dollar amount as they received prior to the bankruptcy of their employer - they receive less. Couple that with the fact that the two largest generations ever seen in this country are now getting ready to retire in droves. What will happen to many of them?

The Third storm has to do with the continuing drop of R.O.I. on investments. The stock market may be in the 10,000 range - but the dividends paid out do not jive with the value of the stock. Ultimately, the stock values will go down. A derivative of the drop of the R.O.I. will also occur in the housing industry. There IS another crash coming in this market. I was a building contractor during the ones that occurred in 1974, 1981, and 1991. Anyone in this industry for more than 12 or 15 years will attest to the fact that these 'crashes' are a reoccurring event. And most will also tell you that these 'crashes' corrected for overvaluation brought about during the good years. What many will also tell you is that once the crash occurs - that as in the past, the market will become vibrant once more, and money will be there to be made. This is a conclusion that all the information I have at hand says is <u>fallacious</u>! Due to deflation, people will have LESS money to spend on the purchase of a home - NOT more. With the Boomer population slowly disappearing, more homes will be available, and thus supply will increase, with a decrease in demand, so prices will go down. We will also witness the disappearance of the Middle Class; this truth is now being touted in the National media, by government leaders.

Sidebar: Throughout the 1920s a long boom took stock prices to peaks never before seen. From 1920 to 1929 stocks more than quadrupled in value. Many investors <u>became convinced that stocks were a sure thing and</u> <u>borrowed heavily</u> to invest more money in the market. Ultimately, they did not have the money to pay on what they had borrowed. This same process is occurring in the real estate market. Homes, over the past ten years, have more than doubled in value, people have used their home as a credit line, and many bought more real estate, assuming that they could continue to do the same. A friend told me that a home purchased three months ago for some $239,000, in the latest release of homes by the same developer, now sells for $270,000 - with no changes in upgrades!

CONNECTING THE DOTS:

Seems like one heck of a storm is already in full brew. All we will wait for is the time of confluence - and that might be sometime after the election. But, these three storms seemingly have no way of being extinguished. Those that will live well (in the Land of Too Much Money) will do so only due to having residual income - just as Robert Kiyosaki teaches. Cash flow will dictate who lives well - not how much money one has (unless one has ten's of millions of dollars!). Those that will live much less well will no doubt just have a job - or multiple jobs. Income created by the trading of one's time for money will not yield the lifestyle most people desire. Cash flow will. There is a business that has the ability to enable one to live in the Land of Too Much Money - you just have to use it!

Find your Passion - it lies either in your Dream(s) - or in your Nightmare/s (whether you are living it or see it coming!). Use your Passion to fuel yourself to do something in your business each day. Remember, the way you live in the next few years WILL be decided by the decisions you make today. Choose well!!!

Remember;

Knowledge is Power;
BUT ONLY INFORMATION IF IT IS NEVER USED!

See All of you Tuesday night at the Radisson - and hear from one who lives in the Land of Too Much Money!

Ross

Chapter One: January 2004
Week Four

Hi again to all of you!

This 'issue' of Money Talk will be a bit different from the normal format.

I would imagine that most, if not all, of you have seen the movie titled The Perfect Storm - or at least know that it is based upon a true occurrence. In a nutshell, a fishing boat found itself caught out at sea at the point of confluence of three big storms - creating what was to be called 'The Perfect Storm'. One that no one had ever seen before - or maybe had even occurred. So you can guess that this was one big, hairy, scary, terrible storm. What I now share is my vision of another 'Perfect Storm'.

It would appear that, economically speaking, there is another Perfect Storm brewing - the confluence of three major economic challenges that are afoot as I write.

The First storm has to do with the issue of Deflation. Wages continue to stagnate;worker unions seem to be more preoccupied with creating stronger health benefits than increasing wages. Jobs continue to disappear - in December it was reported that only 1,000 jobs were created in the entire United States! That is 20 jobs created per State (on average). Jobs continue to go overseas, manufacturing continues to move overseas, and wages in many cases seem to be going down (if one's wage does not go up each year, then by the nature of inflation, the wages really went down - weaker spending power). Prices, in many cases, are also going down - witness the power of Wal-Mart. Margins of profit are either frozen, or in decline.

The Second storm has to do with the issue of Pensions. As noted before, cumulatively - corporate pension plans are some $350 Billion in arrears of being fully funded. Congress is currently working on decreasing the amount that corporations must fund to - making the fund weaker, not stronger. Many of the same issues that pension plans are facing today are close to the same that the Savings and Loan industry faced back in 1989. In fact, '89 was an election year - just as this is an election year (Presidential in both!); the challenges were known - but not talked about - and definitely not addressed - until after the election year. The S & L mess cost the taxpayers of the U.S. in excess of $200 Billion. The branch of the U.S. Gov't that takes over pension plans of bankrupt companies had a $9 Billion surplus three years ago; today it is some $9 Billion in the HOLE! And the hole is getting larger. When the Gov't does take over the bankrupt pension plans, the beneficiaries do NOT receive the same dollar amount as they received prior to the bankruptcy of their employer - they receive less. Couple that with the fact that the two largest generations ever seen in this country are now getting ready to retire in droves. What will happen to many of them?

The Third storm has to do with the continuing drop of R.O.I. on investments. The stock market may be in the 10,000 range - but the dividends paid out do not jive with the value of the stock. Ultimately, the stock values will go down. A derivative of the drop of the R.O.I. will also occur in the housing industry. There IS another crash coming in this market. I was a building contractor during the ones that occurred in 1974, 1981, and 1991. Anyone in this industry for more than 12 or 15 years will attest to the fact that these 'crashes' are a reoccurring event. And most will also tell you that these 'crashes' corrected for overvaluation brought about during the good years. What many will also tell you is that once the crash occurs - that as in the past, the market will become vibrant once more, and money will be there to be made. This is a conclusion that all the information I have at hand says is fallacious! Due to deflation, people will have LESS money to spend on the purchase of a home - NOT more. With the Boomer population slowly disappearing, more homes will be available, and thus supply will increase, with a decrease in demand, so prices will go down. We will also witness the disappearance of the Middle Class; this truth is now being touted in the National media, by government leaders.

Sidebar: Throughout the 1920s a long boom took stock prices to peaks never before seen. From 1920 to 1929 stocks more than quadrupled in value. Many investors became convinced that stocks were a sure thing and borrowed heavily to invest more money in the market. Ultimately, they did not have the money to pay on what they had borrowed. This same process is occurring in the real estate market. Homes, over the past ten years, have more than doubled in value, people have used their home as a credit line, and many bought more real estate, assuming that they could continue to do the same. A friend told me that a home purchased three months ago for some $239,000, in the latest release of homes by the same developer, now sells for $270,000 - with no changes in upgrades!

CONNECTING THE DOTS:

Seems like one heck of a storm is already in full brew. All we will wait for is the time of confluence - and that might be sometime after the election. But, these three storms seemingly have no way of being extinguished. Those that will live well (in the Land of Too Much Money) will do so only due to having residual income - just as Robert Kiyosaki teaches. Cash flow will dictate who lives well - not how much money one has (unless one has ten's of millions of dollars!). Those that will live much less well will no doubt just have a job - or multiple jobs. Income created by the trading of one's time for money will not yield the lifestyle most people desire. Cash flow will. There is a business that has the ability to enable one to live in the Land of Too Much Money - you just have to use it!

Find your Passion - it lies either in your Dream(s) - or in your Nightmare/s (whether you are living it or see it coming!). Use your Passion to fuel yourself to do something in your business each day. Remember, the way you live in the next few years WILL be decided by the decisions you make today. Choose well!!!

Remember;

KNOWLEDGE IS POWER;
BUT ONLY INFORMATION IF IT IS NEVER USED!

See All of you Tuesday night at the Radisson - and hear from one who lives in the Land of Too Much Money!

Ross

Chapter One: January 2004
Week Five

Greetings to all of you!!!

I have to say, I am really 'chomping at the bit' to get this weeks issue out. The news has been on the light side, economically speaking, although there is one headline I wish to address. What I feel led to do is to share the basis of information and thought that is the foundation of the thoughts that I pass on via Money Talk.

The Basis:

1. Inflation: as Mac has so many times demonstrated, this economic vector has been alive and well since 1913. Additionally, it is still alive and well - and will continue to impact our lives. If one researches the inflationary spiral, one will find that back in the early 1900's, the job DID work. The 'husband' typically worked, the 'wife' raised the kids - this is the lifestyle that I grew up in. About the 1960's, inflation mandated the necessity of two incomes - thus the wives went to work in numbers not witnessed before (the number of woman that worked during WW II was mandated only due to the fact that the men were off to War - once the War was over, they came home from work and the man took their place.). What I believe obscured the issue of inflation was the emergence of the NOW movement (National Organization of Woman) - where the tenet of ' a woman can do what any man can do ' became prominent (please do not feel that I say this in a chauvinist way - I see it just as a fact) - and woman

15

thus had a 'reason' to join the work force; thus the <u>real</u> reason for women joining the work force was never understood. The basis of this change was economically directed - a family could not live on one income any longer. Today, we hear that many families now have 2 1/2, or 3 incomes to make it through. If we look back on history, we see that at the beginning of the Industrial Age, one income did the job; then two incomes were necessary, and today 3 or more. If one were to 'plot' (mathematically speaking) the number of jobs required to sustain a family over time, one would witness a curve - no doubt a curve that would be exponential (kinda like the inflationary curve!). Thus, during shorter and shorter periods of time, more jobs (read that as ' income sources ') will be required. Inasmuch as most people can handle no more than two jobs, multiple incomes WILL demand income from MULTIPLE sources (whoa baby!!! What type of business can do that?)

2. History of the Ages: If one researches the time at which the Agrarian Age (also known as the Agricultural Age) disappeared, and the Industrial Age was born (about 1740's in England, 1900's in America), one will witness how the creation of lifestyle changed at the same time. Ultimately, one will see that that manner in which ' lifestyle ' was created in the older Age died during the birth of the new Age. The Industrial Age, with its' birth', also gave life to new mechanics of lifestyle generation. It was during the Industrial Age that words such as ' job, vacation, retirement, return-on-investment ' were borne into our lexicon (vocabulary). Now that we are more and more fully into the Information Age, one will witness the destruction (death) of these 'processes' (formed during the Industrial Age) and the birth of new processes, fully acclimated to this new Age. For it can be seen that processes created by an Age work only in that Age. Thus, retirement will cease to exist (or even come into existence) for many, job security will completely disappear (maybe has already!); and diminution of R.O.I. will be the ultimate driver of change.

(For a fuller description of the changes brought about during the birth of the Industrial Age, one might get a copy of The Worldly Philosophers.)

3. History: It has been written that those that do not learn from the past are doomed to repeat the past. Indeed, from my perspective, influenced both by age and reading, life could be said to be cyclical in nature (no pun intended there!). There is a humongous number of books and articles in print that exhibit our economical past, and forecast our future. Just as eating too much and having little or no exercise usually leads to a state of obese ness (though does NOT mandate that outcome - that outcome is an expected result), economical challenges that are repeated usually bring about the same, or near same, economical results. As I have written before, there are some very scary parallels between the 1933 'crash' and the economic climate today. And close parallels between the S&L debacle of the early 1990's and our pension plan funding of today.

Now, the article that I find in today's Sacramento Bee:

'A Nation of Alfred E. Neumans with nary a worry ': In essence, this article decries the fact that our Government acts just like most people, economically speaking. For the past several decades, we have been going more into debt each year, but just bit-by-bit (4% - 6%/year). Eventually, the debt will catch up to us, personally, and as a Nation. Being as the U.S. is the largest debtor nation in the world, many countries out there are starting to sell of U.S. currency - which will put more and MORE U.S. currency into play - which will fuel inflation. A bond sell-off could destroy the housing market, and our financed-based economy will slow down. And no one seemingly is too worried about this. (Factor this action with what you know about deflation!)

CONNECTING THE DOTS:

What I shared as my 'basis' is just an overview of what fuels my Passion for building my business. There are so many other issues that I have come to understand that time/space does not allow me to write about - yet would be just as impactful to the topic.

If one had a ticket for a first class cabin on an ocean liner named the Titanic, and though some process came to understand the 'probable' future of this ship, would one ever get on? And if already on, would one do all that one could do to get off? In ' my world ' - and it is MY WORLD (formed by my 'truths') - our economy is sailing on the Titanic. Gloom and Doom - no way. What I have learned is that with every cloud, there IS a silver lining! For every action, there is an opposite reaction. For an economic downturn for some, there is an economic upturn available for others - one just has to see what one has to do (not usually what one WANTS to do, either!). For more on this, see The Common Denominator of Success, by Albert E.N. Gray. Oh, I see massive changes in our economic future, the way business WILL be conducted, and I see many that will lose - but many that will win. It will all come down to one word: CHOICE! The biggest challenge with e-mail is that I cannot convey (even using CAPS!) the energy and enthusiasm I feel as I write this. My Friends, change WILL come, and that is the good news! The even better news is that you have the ability to CHOOSE how you will live in the future - it truly is ALL ABOUT YOU!!! The law of Nature that states "help enough people get what they want and you will get what you want "is alive and well. {That is a close parallel to the Golden Rule - and I mean the REAL Golden Rule: Do unto others.... (Sermon over).}

As for Connecting the Dots in regard to the article I cited, this is YOUR job today! For your Truths are your Reality.

And if you would, take a minute and let me know how you 'connected the dots' - I would truly love to hear from you.

In conclusion, I write (and will continue for the foreseeable future) this column due to the fact that my business is one of 'Teaching'. My 'job' - if you will, is to share information - but not as a 'teacher' - for it is written that to be successful in teaching another: " Men must be taught as if you taught them not, And things unknown proposed as things forgot." [Alexander Pope - from How to Win Friends and Influence People by Dale Carnegie.]

GO!   SHARE!!   TEACH!!!

Each of you have Seeds of Greatness in you - feed and water them - and become GREAT!!!

In Service To You,

Ross

Oh, and don't forget:

Knowledge is Power
but if not used - only information.

Chapter Two: February 2004

Good Morning - Afternoon - Evening (you check the one that applies)!!!

Here it is, the day after the first Business Function of the 2004 year. And if you are like me, then you are really ready to get to the action of building YOUR BUSINESS faster than you were just last month (one day ago!). And the emphasis of this function seemed to be: find your WHY!!! First and foremost, we each need to find the 'why' - that special 'why' that will enable us (push us?) to do that which so many others will not do. I heard a speaker talk about how someone's dream might be 'stolen'. Can a 'dream' really be stolen? Or is it more likely that the dream was more of a 'wish'? The fundamentals which constitute the basis of my dream I expressed in a recent Money Talk - my dream will become my reality - and I know yours will too. Forgive me if what I just expressed is not what you would expect in this venue - but this Business Function got me to thinking on an even deeper plane. Now on to business:

1. Jobless aid fund in danger: The state (California) will run out of cash to pay jobless benefits this year - and will borrow hundreds of millions from the federal government. Now, legislative leaders are questioning the structure of the tax system that underpins the fund. (Sacto. Bee, 29 Jan 2003).

2. Senate OK's bill reducing firms' pension liability: The Senate passed a bill that will reduce by $96 Billion payments

companies will have to make into their pension plans this year and next. "Our pension plans are being battered by a perfect storm of declining interest rates, stock market declines and a weak economy", said Sen.. Edward Kennedy, D-Mass. The "bill will help the hard-earned pensions of millions of Americans to weather this storm." (Hey, who forwarded my column of 01.18.04 to Ed?) The PBGC (Pension Benefit Guaranty Corp) took over 152 bankrupt pension plans last year and saw its deficit rise to a record $11.2 Billion. (Sac Bee, 01.29.04)

3. Economists find job market date hard to pin down (Sac Bee, 01.30.04): What do you do when it is unclear what the job market is doing?

4. Job ad revenue down: (Sac Bee, 01.30.04). Help wanted ad revenue fell 6.6 percent in the fourth quarter. "This is an important revenue category for us and it has been down for quite a while in the recession."

CONNECTING THE DOTS:

1. Let's say you have a friend who has a bunch of credit cards (all of them maxed out) and not enough income to make all the payments. And he comes to you to ask you to lend him money enough to make payments for the next year. Yet, you too have all your cards maxed out - and making payments is becoming a chore. Do you lend him your money? This seems to be what the State of California is asking the U.S. Government. Does that make any economic sense at all?

2. This pension challenge is NOT going to go away! Based upon this action by the Senate, pension plans will now be over $450 Billion in the hole - that is almost $1/2 Trillion Dollars!!!!! And that does not even include the State pension plans - which are funded in much the same manner as the private funds. A question: did anyone come out alive that

found themselves in that 'Perfect Storm'? While this storm cannot take lives - it surely can take 'lifestyle'.

3. & 4. Maybe they should just read the paper? Ad revenue is down for the McClatchy publishing empire - and this would no doubt be true for all publishing enterprises that print ads for job listings. To meet this trend, publishing firms must either lower the billing cost for advertising the jobs, reduce the pay of those that take these ads, lower bonuses or increase the bounds for bonuses, or - hire English speaking people over seas to take the ads and really cut the cost they presently incur. (Do the people that are hired in India get SSS, or sick leave, or 401 plans?). Jobs, nonetheless, continue to be in a diminishing supply here in America.

In conclusion, it has been written that the Fed might raise interest rates in the foreseeable future since deflation is not around any longer (do you seriously believe that statement?) - and there might be a chance for inflation to come back. The process of working for advanced degrees online is being advertised continuously on the Internet - yet education in and of itself CANNOT generate lifestyle any longer - continuous income will define the type of lifestyle any of us have. My ' Dream ' is to escape the economic ' nightmare ' that is coming - to live in the land that Robert Kiyosaki calls The Land of Too Much Money. The alternative, The Land of Too Little Money, is just not appealing - since I have been there, done that!

This is a new month my friends - set your goals, write them down and work towards them! Do NOT become one of the 'mediocre' - for they will not live in the land of Too Much Money. Choose wisely!

Remember:

KNOWLEDGE IS POWER;
IF NOT USED IT IS JUST INFORMATION

Ross

Chapter Two: February 2004
Week Two

Hello to all you fellow travelers on the road to economic freedom!!!

Just finished a conversation with a business associate who has had some real tough monetary challenges set before her during the past three months. Her mother, who lives in a Southern State, came down with a lung infection. As it turns out, this particular State demands to know where payment for hospital services will come from. No source of payment - no medical service! Thus, the economic demands fell to this associate and her sisters. During this struggle, she did find one more reason for building her business. And this true story is a segue into the first article I have to share with you.

1. Retiree Health Benefit Slashed (Sacto. Bee, 02.08.04): Employers have unleashed a new wave of cutbacks in company paid health benefits for retirees, with a growing number of companies saying that retirees can retain coverage ONLY if they are willing to bear the full cost themselves.

2. Philly foreclosure crisis (Sacto.Bee, 02.07.04): With a record number of Philadelphia homeowners unable to pay their mortgages, city officials are trying to convince a judge to suspend the city's foreclosure auctions. "This is the worst time for foreclosures since the Great Depression," said John Dodds, director of the Philadelphia Unemployment Project. This week saw a record 1,120 homes up for bid. The national

rate of homes in foreclosure peaked at a record 1.2 percent of all mortgages in the first quarter of 2003.

3. Listen Up! The Fed does speak English (Wall Street Journal, 02.08.04): On Wednesday morning, the voice of Alan Greenspan will start echoing through a cavernous hall on Capitol Hill. All over the world, traders and business executives will listen for one thing: will the Federal Reserve chairman hint as to when the Fed will raise rates.

Connecting the Dots:

1. Companies can no longer afford to pay for health plans for their retirees. As everyone is aware of, medical costs rise faster than inflation (even the real inflation rate!) - we see yearly raises in the double digit area!!! It will soon be that no company will offer any medical/health plans - they will become the responsibility of the individual. Just one more item to fund from one's 401/IRA/whatever plan. But, if it is true (as it is) that people are finding it tough to adequately fund for the living portion of retirement, how much more tough will it be to fund in health also? And those that seek refuge in the fact that their plan 'promises free health plans' - even those in the public sector (teachers/state workers and such) will find the rules changed! If the money is not there, then does it make sense that the rules will have to be changed?

2. Foreclosures in Philadelphia!!! When we find happenings such as this in Middle America, where home costs are no where as high as they are in California, then something must be happening. Does it follow that when these homes were purchased that the buyers were qualified? They had jobs that created income that covered the necessities as deemed necessary by the lenders to qualify them. Today, that income must have either been lost, or that the buying power of their money has diminished. It is true today that the income of a

25

job lost is usually not restored in the finding of a new job - the income is usually less. Jobs going overseas will contribute to this trend. And, with inflation still at 6% a year or more, and wages either stagnant or going down, discretionary income/ buying power of money also diminishes. And, with the cost of homes in California as they are, there will come a 'bust' in the building industry - and as I have written before - I believe that this 'bust' will never witness a rebound. Deflation is alive and well!

3. Strange, isn't it, that so many Leaders of Commerce are seeking direction from one man. Alan Greenspan seemingly has more economic clout than maybe any other one man in the World. It goes without saying, that most CEO's always try to find what the majority are doing - then they do it. Leadership? Or is it just trying to stay in the middle of things?

Alan Greenspan is somewhere in his 70's, as I remember. I raise this fact, not to insinuate that he is senile, rather to ask: is it possible that since he was raised, lived, and schooled in the Industrial Age, that he might not be as quick to see the changes that the Information Age will bring? Or, could it be that he does see the changes, but does not wish to unleash his feelings for fear of what reaction the business world would take? At any rate, the Age we are in will bring about many changes, and quickly. We are already witness to the loss of jobs in America, going overseas (the Global Village concept of Marshall McLuhan). High tech computer jobs have thousands clamoring for the same position - thus rendering them lower paying by 100% than just five years ago. We are witness to companies filling bankruptcy in numbers as never before. We witness pensioners having to go back to work - even after working for 30 years! We witness the diminishing R.O.I. on investments. We witness change in almost every venue of life. Change is static! (Might that be an oxymoron?)

What will the prudent individual do, who recognizes that change is occurring faster each day? Will s (he) keep doing what was done in the past, or seek to find a new path? Remember, in life the norm is mediocrity - the 'middle', if you will. Yet, life is changing in America such that there will be no middle (class, anyway) - just those that live in the land of Too Little Money or in the land of Too Much Money. Your pick!

Remember:

KNOWLEDGE IS POWER;
BUT INFORMATION ONLY IF NOT USED

Take care, and have a Fabulous Week!!!

Ross

Chapter Two: February 2004
Week Three

Happy Valentines to all of you out there who are headed to the Land of Too Much Money!!!

What is Valentine Day all about, you say?

As I learned it when I was but a young lad {(boy, sounds like I grew up during the last Century!) - (Whooops - I did grow up in the last Century!!! But, not in the early part of the Century, when they called young men 'lads')} - I determined that this 'special' day was about letting that very 'special someone' in your life know that you still cared. In that vein, did you send yourself a card? For although we acknowledge others of whom we care deeply about, should we not also care deeply about our self? And would it make sense to say, "Yes, I do care about my self" - since one part of the reason you (as a reader of this column) are building YOUR business is so that YOU can live the way YOU really want to? And of course, to help change the lives of others that you also care deeply about.

So: HAPPY VALENTINE!!!

Now, on to the news:

1. America's trade deficit ballooned to an all-time high in 2003 of $489.4 Billion, 17.1% higher than in 2002 (the previous record), so stated the Commerce Department.

2. Toy Makers challenge giant Wal-Mart (Sacto. Bee; 02.14.04); Led by W/M, discount retailers won a war with

other toy stores this past holiday season. Now, toy makers, a casualty in that bitter fight, have decided to make their own stand. To protect themselves and toy retailers they see as key to their profits, some manufacturers plan to deliver fewer hot toys to W/M and have more exclusive launches at chains like Toys-R-Us. W/M is a very important part of the toy business, but toy makers don't want its low-pricing strategies to devalue their brands and their business - and put more toy retailers out of business, so stated Jim Silver, publisher of the Toy Book, and industry magazine.

3. The Brain Drain (Sacto. Bee; 02.15.04); In essence, this article (which I would suggest you find and read) is about the Brain Drain that America is experiencing in the film industry. In particular, the Lord of the Rings trilogy, which was shot in New Zealand, brought in hundreds (if not thousands) of people from around the world to make this movie. And, Peter Jackson (director) is now planning of making a re-make of the King Kong movie at a cost of some $150 Million dollars - in New Zealand! Not just in the arena of movies, but of science and other business venues, business is being set up internationally.

4. On the George Stephanopoulos (sorry if spelled incorrectly) program - Sunday AM - 02.15.04; A panel made up of economists, businessmen, legislators spoke to the issue of job out-sourcing overseas.

CONNECTING THE DOTS:

1. America is the largest debtor nation in the world - most are aware of this - yet pay little attention to the possible ramifications this debt can bring to us as a Country, and thus to us as individuals. If you are a debtor, than is it true that the one holding your IOU can wield a certain power over you? Not so sure that is true? Then, what would occur if you did not make

your car payment for the next 90 days? Might someone, in the dead of night, hook it up to a tow-truck and drag it away? Or, what about your house payment? Try not making that for 3 or 4 months - what would happen? So, all these countries have IOU's - in the form of bonds - and they decide to dump them and get their money - and could that lead to inflation? And, coupled with the decline of wage increases, could that fit the definition of 'deflation'?

2. This ties into the article I reported on 11.30.03 (W/M rivals girding for a fight) - in which W/M is seen as a challenge to many industries. Clorox, which sells some 30% of its product to W/M - is in the same boat as the toy manufacturers. While a manufacturing company may exude in large volume sales to one outlet, if that outlet ultimately destroys smaller outlets and becomes more powerful, would that manufacturing firm ultimately come under control, indirectly, of that outlet? This 'challenge' is also seen in the continuing strike by the retail union down in Southern California - which is now in its fourth month! Can you imagine not getting a paycheck for four (4!!!) months??? Oh, remember item 1. above? Do you think that those that work at W/M make less than those that did work at Ralph's, Von's, or Safeway? So, do these workers ultimately settle for less - and go back to work - or find their jobs gone - and find work somewhere else - for less? Who looses? Maybe those that give the responsibility for their lives to someone else? For in giving 100% power to your job, is not the business boss/owner taking responsibility for your lifestyle? Stay tuned for future updates in this struggle.

3./4. We 'live' in a Global Village - anyone that doubts that has most likely not paid attention to the headlines, heard the news - or lost his/her job yet. Jobs WILL continue to go overseas - for how does a government outlaw that action? Remember a few years ago when a major issue was the bringing in of immigrants to the US with special work visa's? I hear that the demand is now down by over 50%! Why? The reason is in front of you - the Internet! If you owned a business in which you paid your US employee $50,000 a year (benefits included), but which you could find a worker in another country could do the same job for only $25,000 a year - what would you do? And if you had stock holders that wanted larger returns on their investment, what would you do? Change is inevitable - we are just starting to move into the Information Age - and Global employees are just a part of it. What the panelists on the G.S. show stated was that we are in the midst of radical change - and the consensus they hold is that there is NO consensus on what it will do and how it will play out.

Side-bar: I was talking to a young man I have known for several years when I was on Jury Duty. He currently works for one of the larger banks in Sacramento - and I asked him how he wished to live in the next five years. His reply was that he liked his job (working with depositors via phone/internet) and would continue there. When I asked him about the possibility of outsourcing - he made a statement to the effect that his job could not be done in that manner. What I would ask is this: would it make sense to any banking institution to employ someone with a little college education, spend $40,000 or more a year to keep him; or to hire a business degree-d graduate, maybe with an MBA, for only $25,000 a year? After all, the only contact is made via phone/internet.

Another friend was enrolled in the Microsoft program (or something akin to that) that he had paid almost $2000 to take. He started his own Internet business; and literally walked away from the rest of the tech program. Today, we witness a mass surplus of computer tech's - so many so that the pay is less today than it was five years ago. That field is now further eroded by those well educated in foreign lands - ready and willing to work for less than is paid here in the United States.

My friends, as I have stated before (and no doubt will again), education no longer assures anyone of a solid financial future. Sad to say, cash flow is the only way to stay financially fit. And the more cash flow one can create, the more solid the life-style - and the best cash flow is the residual cash flow. The coming months will usher in changes like not seen before - please do not hesitate to build YOUR future today! You have both the vehicle and the motor - you build your own chassis!

Remember:

KNOWLEDGE IS POWER;
IF NOT USED, IT IS MERELY INFORMATION!

Ross

Chapter Two: February 2004
Week Four

Greetings and Salutations!!!

Here we sit, another week 'under the belt' - ever wonder what that phrase really means? I have absolutely NO clue, but if you do, please be so kind as to share your knowledge with me and I will put it out to all of our readers.

Ah....... Knowledge. Just what is 'knowledge'? Webster defines 'knowledge' as "familiarity gained by actual experience." Is it not true that 'actual experience' can also be 'history'? Experience of others, not of our own - yet experience, nonetheless. Thus, the quote that we have heard: ' those that do not learn from History are doomed to repeat it' - is a truth, for is not a 'history' of anything an 'experience', and thus qualifies as KNOWLEDGE? Where am I going with this? No idea as of yet, but I do know it will weave into my final conclusions for this issue!

1. Medical uncertainty for retirees (Sacto. Bee;02.17.04): Sacramento County supervisors consider cutting medical insurance subsidies for retirees by a third. Since 1980, the county has given its retirees a subsidy for medical insurance, but is now experiencing a monetary shortfall, due to three years of stock market losses (and the loss of a costly court case involving retirees). County staff recommended cutting the subsidy by a third, to $163 a month; the average pensioner takes home $1393 a month, after taxes. Some supervisors want to cut the subsidy off 100%, noting that "...we are frankly running out

of money." Judy Cook, widow of a retiree, stated " ...retirees need the entire medical subsidy. It's bad policy when a governing board lays down its responsibility to people who have given their working lives to this county."

2. Steel prices soar 66% in a world market 'gone mad' (USA Today; 02.20.04): Shortage fears are leading to a rapid rise in steel prices, squeezing U.S. manufacturers already reeling from a deep three-year downturn. For U.S. consumers, the rising cost will have little impact - but for the manufacturing sector, which has already lost 2.2 million jobs in the past three years, it feels like insult added to injury. Jody Fledderman, president of Batesville Tool and Die, a firm that makes parts for the auto industry: " It's already so difficult in this business, a lot of people are starting to think there has got to be a better way to make a living."

3. Businesses' fees may jump (Sacto. Bee; 02.21.04): The Sacto. Board of Supervisors will consider changes to its business licensing program, raising fees and requiring an estimated 6,000 businesses that have been allowed to operate without licenses to obtain them. The changes are expected to raise $1.4 million, allowing the County to beef up its code inspectors by adding two more office staff members and two field inspectors. Although facing budget cuts this year, officials say expanding the license fee is not a bid to raise money for the general fund - only to cover the cost of the program.

4. Grocery clerks look south, see threat to way of life (Sacto Bee, 02.22.02): Northern Calif supermarket workers are feeling the effects of the largest supermarket strike in history - months before their own contract expires. Many are putting aside extra dollars and delaying major expenditures, fearing a drawn out dispute would leave them in a financial pinch. "It's terrifying. I couldn't afford to be out of a job. You try to save what you can." Long time employees are especially

worried about their retirement benefits. "People are really worried about what their benefits are going to be like and how much of their retirement is going to be left."

CONNECTING THE DOTS:

1. It is not too hard to empathize with the feelings of those retired people; they worked hard, gave up much of their life, for the promises of employment, and especially - retirement, benefits. The saddest part of it all is that the retirees are worried about losing $84.00 +/-!!! In this day and age, do many of us worry too much about $84.00? Probably not, but think to the future, when you might be on a fixed income and everything is going up - $84.00 takes on a much added significance. Again, less than $100.00. Is this a sad state of affairs, or what?

2. On top of this, with the dollar devaluation in Europe, fewer Americans are going over there to vacation - which now hurts the European industry! So, steel costs go up here in America (where the steel industry has been losing firms like crazy!), which ultimately will drive up the cost of steel-required products we buy here (inflation), yet wages remain stagnant - and jobs continue to get 'lost' overseas (combined, does this reek of deflation?).

3. Ok, it may be that I am in error, but if you raise taxes to the tune of $1.4 million a year, hire four people - and just break even - then my math indicates that the average cost for each of these four new 'hires' comes to $350,000.00 a year! Now, don't jump to conclusions - obviously health and retirement benefits also must come out of this $350,000.00 - so the wages could not be more than $250,000.00 a year (If you do not hear from me in the future - it might be because I got one of these four really nice paying jobs!!!). Hope you got a good laugh out of that last statement - I did!!! So, is it possible that

they made a small mistake and some of that money really will find its way into the general fund?

4. Ah, the continuing saga of the grocery market strike down South. Friends, if anything could wake us up, it has got to be this issue that we continue to see drag on. Realize that this is really for 'all the marbles'! Whoever loses, loses for all time - it is about the Unions vs. Corporate America. Corporate America cannot afford what it has given, or been won by the Unions, in the past. R.O.I. will not allow them to do so. I am of the understanding that only about 13% of American workers belong to a union - and that most of them are government workers. The Unions were a part of the Industrial Age, for the Industrial Age (manufacturing, in particular) required much human labor. Today, less labor - and definitely cheaper labor. R.O.I. is a concept developed in the Industrial Age - a concept that is seemingly becoming more and more outmoded by the emergence of the Information Age - where information is the paramount commodity - not labor. In a world where the power of money is seemingly the most powerful fuel to change, expect to see the workers lose; both the battle and the war. The corporations are united, as are the strikers; but the corporations have the largest monetary resources - and can thus outlast the strikers. Also, there are those who lost jobs elsewhere (maybe their job went overseas?), and finding any job would be better than no job at all.

Change is coming - expect it, plan for it, but do not allow change to cause pain in your life by not building the one business that can defeat the changes that must come - YOUR business!!!

You are witness to the creation of 'knowledge' - the challenges that those who trusted in an old system face today when they cannot really work any longer - yet must live with the consequences of their decisions: putting their trust (and really control of their lives, in someone else's hands. You are witness to both inflation and wage stagnation occurring simultaneously (deflation). You are witness to 'leaders' calling for protectionist laws (similar to what helped cause the Great Depression). You are witness to the increasing need for government to raise taxes - look at California and say we need no new taxes. And lastly, you are witness to the dismantling of organized labor, for labor is not at the forefront any longer. You are witness to ongoing truths - and thus, you now have Knowledge. When using your 'knowledge' in determining when and why to build your business, do as the old Crusader (the one in Indiana Jones and the Last Crusade) said: " Choose wisely!"

Remember,

Knowledge is Power;
but if not used, it is only information!

Yours in Choosing Well!!!

Ross

Chapter Two: February 2004
Week Five

End of Month - and it really is the 'end of the month'!

Did you hit your goal for business volume? Maybe a better question would be: ' Did you set a goal for business volume?'

What in the world do any of the above questions have to do with this column? As far as I can tell, everything - and nothing. Everything, if you are truly desirous of living 'Large' - nothing, if living as you are is 'OK' with you. If you don't have a target to aim at, how can you tell if you even aimed the right direction? You gotta have a target in sight to know.

Well, using this thought I will segue into the first article:

1. Striking grocery workers approve agreement (Today; 02.29.04) : After a two-day vote, 86% of grocery workers who cast ballots approved the contract negotiated by the United Food and Commercial Workers union, the union said Sunday in a statement. Union leaders said they wanted to protect affordable health care, pensions and job security. "These three goals were accomplished in the new agreement, indicating the workers' struggle and sacrifice were worthwhile," the statement read.

2. Taxpayer, beware: Fannie & Freddie could be our next S&L crisis (Sacto. Bee, 02.29.04); Freddie and Fannie have gotten themselves in big trouble. For those of you who do not follow the business pages, I only wish we were talking about

pregnant teenagers. Fannie and Freddie (Mae and Mac, respectively) are the two government sponsored mortgage companies that help most of us buy homes. Trouble is, they have run themselves into big-time debt: almost $2 Trillion - and done it over the past five years. And look who is on the hook if these things go under: the taxpayers, that is who!

CONNECTING THE DOTS:

1. As I stated in prior columns, this strike was for 'all the marbles' - and I stand by that statement. Yes, the strike is over - and yet, it is also reported that the settlement was not much different from the offer they received in October - four months ago. They now pay more for health care, where before they paid nothing. There is no raises with this contract - one time bonuses for prior time worked - but that can in no way make up for all the monies each employee lost over four months of staying home. The corporations won. Sunny Kin, a service manager at Ralph's, said she was disappointed with the final results, even though she hadn't seen the contract. "Why did we go on strike? I lost a lot of money for nothing. I think the guys were misled," Kim said.

Now watch what happens to the grocery workers here in the North when their contracts expire this Summer. Some union leaders say they will be able to get a better deal - do you really think so? (This whole issue reminds me of that story of the one cow who, unknowingly, is in a crowd of other cows headed to the 'last stop'. This one cow looks up and see's that though all the cows think they are doing well and headed in the right direction, he see's that the cows - one-by-one - are getting hit in the head. Once they get to the front, there is no turning back.) Oh, do you believe that the strikers 'hit their target'? Or did they miss greatly?

2. I have to say that I knew of both these entities: Freddie Mac and Fannie Mae - since I was in the construction industry for 25 years. Yet, I really knew little of what they did. So, I did what you would do: I went to the Internet and did a search, and found out!!! These companies do not really have a 'signed' letter saying that the government stands behind all their loans, but almost everyone believes that the government has to, since they created these entities. The challenge is that because of the hot market that has existed for the past years, their 'possible' indebtedness has grown really large - as reported above, to some $2 Trillion dollars. And, many financial experts have been saying that a crisis could well come. What I did learn is this: one paper, Vol 1, Issue 2, March 2002, of the Fannie Mae Papers had a concluding thought: "...Freddie Mac would require government assistance only in a severe housing market downturn."

During the years 1973 to the present, I have witnessed (and lived through) housing constrictions in 1974, 1981, 1991. Each of these (as memory serves) was brought about by a 'hot' housing market. Especially in 1991, when properties were appreciating double digits - in only several months! The same action is occurring today. But, as I outlined in one of my prior papers, today we live in a 'new' economy - the Information Age economy. In the Industrial Age economy, after each of the above mentioned downturns, the housing market did rebound. My forecast is that when the next one occurs (and it will!), there will be no rebound. Thus, it seems to me that the government will indeed be forced into spending more money to prop up Fannie and Freddie - just as they did to the Savings and Loans - which cost us, the taxpayer, some 1/2 Trillion dollars. This could be even worse. I do not present myself as an expert in this arena, yet I do sense some real challenges coming our way. Taxes would be raised, and government spending would have to decrease (remember what Alan Greenspan just said about lowering spending for SSS?).

Those that have created income NOT dependent on their trading of time for dollars (see article 1, above), and have also created income beyond their monthly needs (see article 2, above) will get through life much easier and comfortably than those that have not. Could this be a reason for each of you to do just a little bit more each month in building your financial future? Only you know that answer.

Remember:

KNOWLEDGE IS POWER:
BUT ONLY INFORMATION IF NOT USED

See ya on the Hi-ways and Bi-ways!

Ross

Chapter Three: March 2004

Happy Spring!!!

What a beautiful day it was today!!! For breakfast I took Linda to breakfast at Tower Cafe - right next to the Tower Theater - for those of you familiar with the Sacramento area. They have outdoor eating - and a 'killer' French (er... Freedom?) Toast!!! If you have not had a chance to have breakfast there, it is one place we would recommend.

Now that the weekly advertisement is done and over with, on with the news!!!

1. Greenspan urges: Fix Social Security (USA Today, 02.26.04); Greenspan has urged Congress to cut the growth of S.S. and Medicare, warning that without action, the nation faces unsustainable deficits, rising long-term interest rates and slow growth in living standards. Raising taxes enough to deal with the deficit problems could hurt the economy, and tax increases would likely be part of any fix.

2. Greenspan says Freddie, Fannie need oversight (USA Today, 02.25.04); Greenspan said Tuesday that mortgage giants Fannie Mae and Feddie Mac could impose a threat to the U.S. financial system unless Congress imposes tighter oversight and limits on their growth. The two GSE's (Government Sponsored Enterprises) own or guarantee $4Trillion in mortgages and have grown into two of the largest financial institutions in the nation. "To fend off possible future systemic

difficulties, which we assess as likely if expansion continues unabated, preventative actions are required sooner than later," Greenspan said.

CONNECTING THE DOTS:

1. This was not the only statements issued concerning Social Security (or as we business people call it, ' Social Insecurity'). Greenspan headed a commission in 1983 that made proposals which formed the core of what was to be a permanent S.S. "fix", which included an increase in the payroll tax. Today he is calling for action to narrow the fiscal deficit before it becomes irreparable. How? By cutting spending: reduce the cost-of-living cost increases, and speed up the age at which Americans can receive full retirement benefits. Many of you may have heard the message that it might be appropriate for those at age 62 (or is it 62 1/2?) to take early benefits, since if you wait until 65, there is a good chance that by then, they will have reduced benefits you would have received at 62! There are many, many workers out there who have never planned on getting much from S.S. at all! Can any of you live on $1500.00 a month - and of course, pay any taxes due on it? Any body who is planning on becoming dependent upon any of the governmental agencies for the security of their retirement may want to look to some other sources for income. The State of California, and America - is truly in debt up to its' 'eyeballs'! And where do governmental agencies look when they need more money? You! And how do they get it? Does 'taxation' sound like the answer? Do you believe you pay too little in taxes today? If so, send Arnold and Greenspan a check - if not, then would it make sense for you to set a plan in motion and take that responsibility yourself? Only two places anyone can depend upon for living 'large' - and retirement: a government - or - you. Who do you trust the most to do the best for you and your family?

2. Amazing, first we hear that Freddie and Fannie are doing the country a service, then we hear that they are doing the country a dis-service. In my last Money Talk, I mentioned that the last conclusion made in a study, indicated that the government would only have to get involved in the case of a drastic downturn. Within that same study though, it was mentioned that if mortgage rates were to go to high, an economic distress would also occur. So, there just may be a greater chance of an economic challenge than is realized by most of us.

All that any of us can do in regards to the above two issues is to be on the watch and see how it plays out. In the end, is it not in each of our hands as to how we live, no matter what happens? By now we all have quit laughing at that old hack about what 'job' spells: just over broke; we witness it too many times in the lives of people we know and hear about. It is estimated that some 3 million jobs will be out-sourced - and I mean overseas outsourced - while new jobs will be created. With the life span of jobs becoming less than a workers 'work span' - how much sense does it make to go find a new job? And how many times? Would it make sense to just use a job (rather than have a job use you?) to get through the short time, while you build a sounder financial future via your business? Yes, you HAVE TO GO DO SOME WORK!!! But what the heck, you have to go do some work anyway, yes? So, does it make sense to go do a little more work, over a shorter time span, create a financial income dependent upon YOU, who will always be good to you, than to hope in a job? Please do not get me wrong; jobs have a place in everyone's life: but just a short place, not a long one.

Remember:

KNOWLEDGE IS POWER!!!
IF NOT USED, IT IS JUST INFORMATION

See you on the highways and the biways;

Go home when only YOUR porch light is on - and everyone else's is off - and live like you choose to!!!

Ross

Chapter Three: March 2004
Week Two

Howdy All!!!

Hope you have been enjoying this great weather - can you believe it? Over the weekend as I drove by a local hotel I saw people out in the pool area working on their tans!!! And all this time I thought you needed to get over to Hawaii to do that type of thing! Of course, staying local is cheaper than flying to Hawaii - but not nearly as nice - would you agree? All we need is two things: 1) time, and; 2) money. So, maybe this is just one reason, among many, to really work on building your business. Where to work on one's tan!

I only have one article that I wish to comment on this week:

It was reported, in various media, that Warren Buffet has amassed some $36 Billion dollars - that is right, CASH dollars during 2003. No, this is not his personal stash - it is for his companies.

CONNECTING THE DOTS:

Why do you think that Warren would amass such a bundle? Of course one might assume that he is not sticking it in some CD account, since even over three years a CD would yield only about 3%. So again, why might he create such a pile of cash? Thinking back to something I read in one of Robert Kiyosaki's books - I believe that Robert made a comment that money can be made during any economic time

- good or bad. One just has to find the 'silver lining' of the situation. I have felt for some time that the Dow Jones would eventually drop down to 6000 (and there are many others out there that think the same way). Last week I was talking to a group, watching the video where it was stated that Warren believes that the current downturn could last eight years. It was then that I made a possible correlation between his forecast, and his amassing of $36 Billion in cash.

If today some stock sells for $100, yet yields only $3.00 a year in dividends, then the R.O.I. is only 3% - rather sad. But, if that stock went down to $50, and the yield was still $3.00, the R.O.I. goes up to 6%! And, if that stock went down to $25, with a $3.00 yearly dividend, then the R.O.I. would be a really tidy 12%!!! Many out there have written for some time that stocks are over priced, relative to return. The downturn that many forecast would no doubt cause a correction (that is Investee talk) that would re-price stock values. But, this is what I feel is the kicker: With $36 Billion in cash, Warren could then make purchases that would enable him to really enhance his already large empire. And it just epitomizes what Kiyosaki has said so many times: good and bad times always exist; and with each, there is always a way to create wealth.

While most of us (maybe all of us?) do not have the ability to generate even $1 Billion in cash, why not develop a continuing return (annuity?) that such an amount would yield? That is available to each of us; all we need do is to go out and do a little more work. As is always the case in life, it is just a choice!

Remember:

KNOWLEDGE IS POWER;
BUT ONLY INFORMATION IS NOT USED.

Ross

Week Three

What at fantastic week it has been, has it not? Just beautiful weather - sun - trees getting green leaves. Only one small, wee (that is a Scottish word! - learned it from May Mason) challenge: how many of you were just tooooo busy to just go out, drive around and smell the beauty, feel the air - maybe even take in a picnic? Ok, so someone out there reading this is saying ' hey Ross, that is one heck of a run-on sentence'. Yup, you no doubt are correct. But, if you were able to be out there, day in; day out - planning your days 'one-at-a-time', or just 'as-you-went' - due to the fact no one could pay you enough to work for them - would you be able to live a life based upon YOUR whims and desires - not your bosses, or even your businesses??? Just doing what YOU wanted to do! Would life be even better for you? (And if you did live this way, how important is a run-on sentence anyway?)

Uh-oh, got to get back to the real world that most of us live in (Charlie and Christie will save a spot for those of us who want to join them in their world). So, let's see what the headlines brought this past week:

1. Do-it-yourself checkout lanes (Sacto Bee; 03.221.04); 'Mom and daughter then scanned a jar of pickles, a small bag of fresh yams and other groceries through a self-checkout station at an East Sacto Albertson's supermarket. Indeed, consumers increasingly are walking past the traditional staffed checkout lines and heading for space-age, do-it-yourself registers. For supermarkets, it's a critical strategy to stay competitive with non-

union rivals and retail giant Wal-Mart, which has emerged as the nation's No. 1 seller of groceries. A single check-out system saves up to 150 hours a week (journeyman checkout clerks make about $19.00/hr) - nearly four (4) full-time jobs.

2, Media reports on the rising cost of gasoline. We have all seen reports of gasoline possibly hitting the $3.00 per gallon level this year. What does it mean to many?

CONNECTING THE DOTS:

1. Several months ago I was in a local Home Depot and noticed that they had just installed one of these clusters of self-check out registers. There were two or three young ladies (all wearing the standard Orange smock denoting their employee status at H/D) standing around the 'head' register (where they fix challenges coming from the other four registers) and asked them if they were ready to see fewer of their 'herd' working any longer? They immediately told me that the registers were put in to assist customers and that no jobs would be lost; their supervisor/manager told them so. When I shared with them how they did not need the same staffing, they were aghast - surely they would not be told an untruth!

Well, welcome to the 21st Century - for we all will be seeing more of these critters in all of our markets. The Corporate mantra of this Age has to be; ' saving money to raise profits - whatever it takes.' And what it takes is the elimination of repetitive labor; and if you cannot eliminate the labor, then minimize the cost of the labor. Think about it - that is what the Industrial Revolution was all about. Henry Ford created autos via the assembly line - just teach a person one small job, make them efficient, and be able to sell the product cheaper, and make more money via volume. In this Information Age, how about eliminate labor by people, use machines that always show up for work, never demand time off - or - raises!?

Anyone currently employed in the grocery business has to be ready to see massive changes in their work force. Union, or non-union, machines cost less over time. And when one can save some money by using machines vs. people, saving money will most always come out on top. Wal-Mart is coming, and that scares the major grocery chains. Cost efficiency will normally always come out on top; thus the firm that is most cost-efficient will normally always beat out the firm that is less cost-efficient.

2. Gasoline at $3.00 a gallon!!! Sounds like something that can happen rather easily. Have you read that the oil companies are now downsizing the amount of reserves they say they have? Their profitability is based upon their reserves by many investors - and now these companies (Shell, etc) are now saying they have less than they thought. We read that many commuters are saying that if gas goes up a dollar ($1.00) a gallon, they will be in TROUBLE!!! Now, think about this: the average driver probably fills up three, say four times a month. Say, an average of 25 gallons each time. What they are saying is that a change of $100.00 a month in their discretionary spending will create MASSIVE challenges for them. Now, I appreciate the value of a one-hundred dollar bill - but how bad is it when just $100.00 can generate challenges for anyone? That is a sad state of affairs, is it not? Don't get me wrong; I know what it feels like to be in a financial state where a measly $100.00 changes your life - been there, done that. What I have done (with Linda's help) is start moving to a direction where we will not have to re-feel that challenge. Hey, just above this item I noted the case for using machines to save time/money. When is the last time anyone filled your tank? Why? (Probably because there was no-one there to do it for you?) And, how many times have you just 'plugged in your credit/atm card into a machine' and then gassed up - with no interplay with a living being? Friends, this is the world we are coming into - get used to it. And, every time you do some

type of transaction with a real-live human being, give thought to how it might be done with a machine. And know that the time is fast coming when you will see your 'seeing' into the future become a reality!

3. Hey, there is no '3' above - but if we add '1' plus '2' above, I come out with a '3'! Friends, change is coming - and coming faster than probably any of us realize. We go into an election year with the 'job challenge' a number one item. It makes no difference who wins in November - jobs will continue to be lost. We are in the transformational time created by the birth of the Information Age. Ask any Mother; 'does birth cause pain?' - and look out before she hits you with a bat for asking a stupid question! When a birth occurs, new circumstances are generated - demanding new responses. Do you think the average adult (say 21 years of age) who lived during the birth of the Industrial Age found it 'easy'? How hard do you think it was to go from living your life on your time-clock (Agricultural Age) to having to 'go to work - and live by their (Industries) clock'? I think, rather tough - really, really tough! The Information Age is about change. Those that understand that this change is inevitable, and seek out and grab the new processes demanded by this new Age, will prosper (see The Worldly Philosophers - it has already happened once!). Not to beat a dead horse (waste of energy), but I continue to see more and more ads - especially on the internet - espousing getting degrees as the salvation process, financially. Being educated is important - but as the ancient Greeks knew, education is understanding circumstances/situations - and then using that understanding as 'knowledge' of action.

Remember:

KNOWLEDGE IS POWER;
BUT ONLY INFORMATION IF NEVER USED.

Ross

Chapter Three: March 2004

Week Four

Hello to all of You!

And, wasn't the Seminar - hosted last night at the Radisson by David and Karen Waddell (and they always host so well!) for Charlie and Christy Hunt - speaking on Time Management - nothing short of awesome!?! The place was packed; so packed in fact that more chairs were brought in until there was no room for more chairs -so some just had to stand. And the new 'eyes'!!! Linda and I do not remember the last time that a Seminar had any new eyes - let alone the number we had last night. And, to top that off - when it was asked for people to stand that this was their FIRST thingamabob they ever attended - you should have seen that bunch of people. Truly, people are starting to sense that massive changes are occurring in the world of the work - and are seeking an alternative.

Now, for all the news that might not be news in the future:

1. "MY CAT HAS HAIRBALLS!" (Sacto Bee; 03.22.04); If you tell your boss that you won't be coming to work for the day, you're not alone. These days, many employees feel "entitled" to skip work when life's challenges wear them down."It's a mental health day," explained one worker. People are overtly saying that these days, meaning 'I just can't stand it in here!' 'My cat has hairballs' was an excuse actually used; also - 'I can't come into work because my electric garage door will not work'.

2. Overhaul of jobless benefits proposed (Sacto Bee; 03.23.04); A series of bills were rolled out in the state Legislature on Monday intended to overhaul the California unemployment insurance system which, according to state officials, will run out of money this year. Part of the reforms proposed would change eligibility requirements for part-time and low-wage workers, and freeze benefits increases until the system is solvent.

3. Handwriting's On Wall: Soft Quarter (Wall Street Journal; 03.28.04); For the first time in a year, the stock market has run into trouble in recent weeks. All of the major indexes suddenly seem to have hit a ceiling.

4. Many jump into real estate jobs amid boom (Sacto Bee; 03.28.04); Jon Brodie was slipping into a career rut - the landscaping business he started left little family time, and his lack of a college degree limited his career options. Then Jon realized he could sell real estate. Today, he is a full-time real estate agent with a "completely achievable' goal of making $130,000 in annual income.

CONNECTING THE DOTS:

1. Heck, I know people who used that old excuse to not attend a business offering! What is really being stated is that people today are getting tired of the 'job'! Ten years ago the job was a relatively safe 'entity'; people changed jobs because they wanted new challenges, new faces, new places. But, one could actually find a job. If one made, say, $45,000/year - one could most likely find another job paying the same - or even more. Today, that is not the case. We read that employee productivity is at an all time high. Why? Maybe because the average employee is afraid of losing his/her job? If you were an employer, and had people working like crazy, being very productive - would you hire more? Or let the employees pro-

ductiveness make you look like a better manager - by getting more work done for the company, with less money? (Oh, you noticed that that action might save your job too?) I talked to a friend of mine at church this AM, who works in the grocery industry, asking him how he was doing. His reply was ' all the fun is gone. In a couple of years my retirement will be fully vested and I might look to do something else.' Do you not think that most people are thinking the same way?

2. Just great! Here California is already in a financial mess, and now one more 'kid' needs new shoes! Where do you think this money will come from? Only place I can figure, since no one in the Legislature wants to quit spending money, is US!!! Some how, some way, the cost of living in this once great state will go up. Oh, it may not have the word 'taxes' affixed to the process, but they will find other words to do the deed. How about 'fees'? Yeah, 'fees' sounds really good - because not everyone will have to pay that particular fee. But 'fees' can cover so many things. Start reading the fine print in your coming bills. (Oh, have you ever really looked at your last telephone bill? Fully 10% of the bill has to do with taxes, fees, and other stuff.)

3. Again, I see it as the challenge most corporations have in generating consistent, and sizeable, dividends (r.o.i.). One day people will see the stock market, the one they invest in at 'retail', as a poor place to put their hard earned money. How many of your friends, when talking about the market, are saying they are taking their money out? A friend of mine just took out several thousand shares of Intel. I asked him what he would then do with the money? Turned out to be a challenging question - with no current answer. What would you do if you suddenly had several hundred thousand dollars in cash and needed to not only protect it present value, but make its future value exceed the inflationary rate? These are two terms

you all need to become comfortable with: present value and future value.

4. Ah yes, just like the Gold Rush of '49!!! Thousands came to the Sacramento area to find gold. How many did? Very few. Most invested a lot of money, surely their time, and then went home broke (if they made it at all). I have witnessed this scenario before: good times in the housing industry and everyone wants to sell homes, for there is good money for those that do it well. Yet, when the industry goes into its down cycle, only the savvy veterans, the ones with some money put aside, stay. As was with building contractors, new ones show up, old ones pass away (not in the dead sense!). Check out Building Contractors in a Yellow Pages from three years ago: you will find 25% of the names in the old one not in the new one. Yes, today there is money to be made for the individual with a good work ethic and people skills - and a little knowledge of how a house is actually constructed. But, this industry WILL fall, and when it does, it will NOT come back.

Well, I hope this issue brings some things that cause you to think. I am not sure it is one of my better 'lines' - but it is the best I have to offer tonight. I mentioned that I do not see the building industry coming back after it does fall, and maybe I will expand on that thought next week. Or, maybe I will send it out as a 'special thought' during the next couple of weeks - kinda like a 'Special Edition'.

Again, I do not profess to see the future (anymore than Frank Feather does) - only to share with you information that I have put together from numerous sources, in order to get a sense of where we are headed as a country, in the financial realm.

I close with this: an individual e-mailed me last week to say he appreciated my 'Money Talks'.   Now, this individual received it via a friend who receives it. And he asked me how an individual living month to month might live differently in the future. My answer to him, and to you, is: BUILD YOUR INTERNET BUSINESS!!! Don't walk, don't speed walk, don't walk with confidence, don't job, don't run at a fast clip - RUN WITH ALL YOUR MIGHT! And start now. Time is running out on many of us; we feel comfortable with what we have, are making - and do not see it changing overnight. Maybe in the next couple of years, but not too soon. Bad thinking! Get with your Mentor, the one who has the 'pedal to the metal' - and find out how to get your foot there too!!!

Remember:

Knowledge is Power;

BUT ONLY INFORMATION IF NEVER USED.

Yours in Building a Better Tomorrow for each of us and our families!!!

Ross

Chapter Four: April 2004:
Special Edition

I am writing this Special Issue of Money Talk to share some thoughts concerning the Construction/Housing Industry and what I see in the coming days. So, just what do I see?

In a nutshell: it will crash, probably some time after the national elections this November.

CONNECTING THE DOTS:

There is so much that I would share with you on this subject, and I think I may just let it "all out" as it comes to me and not try to write this 'thesis' in a manner that would garner me an 'A' grade from some teacher. So, with that in mind, here it comes.

In a nutshell, there has been too much appreciation, coupled with stagnant wage increases, exasperated by continuing job losses. All this, as I see it, in an economy that is dealing with a deflationary issue. Let me expand on these statements.

The past several years we have seen an economy that seemingly is in a recovery mode. Upon closer scrutiny, we find that this recovery has been fueled largely by consumer spending. Given this fact, what is the economy spending? Money from two sources: credit cards, and refinancing monies. The average person's debt, as a percentage of his income, is now higher that it has ever been. Americans have been using their homes as personal ATM machines. Thus, this new found money has fueled consumer spending and is propping up the American Economy. For the first time, the motor of our economy is not manufacturing (for that was a part of the Industrial Age), but rather an inflated housing market (based upon service industries - a component of the Information Age!). Greenspan is no doubt very well aware that we are sitting on a housing bubble; on a scale only seen once since the Great Depression. Worse, when this inflated housing market bursts, it may well take the economy down with it.

[NOTE: It has been stated that the Information Age will witness the greatest transfer of wealth ever seen in history.]

Good News/Bad News: The 'good news' is that in most of the country there is no housing bubble. In contrasting home prices to annual income, most of the country ranges from 2.1:1 to 2.9:1. Only in 20 metro areas - mostly located in eight states, does this ratio defy logic. The 'bad news' is that those areas contain roughly 50% of the housing wealth of the country. In California, the ratio is 8.3:1; Hawaii is 10.1:1!!! To some extent, supply/demand forces has caused this anomaly. At some point incomes cannot sustain the prices. That point has now been reached. In the late 80's, the last time these eight states saw price/income ratios this high, the real estate market collapsed.

Another measure of the bloated housing market can be seen in the rental arena. One would expect that in an expanding economy, the cost of renting would increase as the cost of a home increases. Yet, we see today that as housing costs expand as they have, the rental market is actually flat, and in some cases, in decline. This gap would give rise to the thought that many buying homes today are doing so as 'speculation'. [Note: during the late, late 80's, (when I was a building contractor) I witnessed a massive increase in home prices. And concurrently, witnessed people buying homes in a tract, still under construction, with the goal of putting them on the market when the next phase for that tract came out. Thus, making a tidy $10-20,000 in a three or four month period! The 'crash' hit us in 1991 (where I live), when homes actually - and for the first time in my lifetime - lost value!]

When the crash comes, many will then want to determine who or what caused it. The answer will point to many. Freddie Mac and Fannie Mae are part of the reason. When the U.S. Government first sponsored Fannie Mae in the 1930's, it was to encourage banks to make loans to low-income Americans, which Fannie Mae would the buy up. In 1970, Freddie Mac was born by Congress, to do much the same thing as Fannie Mae. By the late 80's, they were buying up to 30% of these mortgages and then repackaging them as securities. But, they had a challenge before them: they were severely limited in their ability to attract investment capital. Then, Congress made some subtle changes in their charge that made them more attractive to investors. Also, bank regulators allowed pension plans and mutual funds classify Fannie Mae and Freddie Mac as 'low risk'. During the 1990's, investors were throwing money at Freddie and Fannie, which became enormously profitable. The price-cap on these mortgages were raised, until today they now fund middle and upper-middle class mortgages - whereas they originally had been created to help the low-income class. And the share of the nations mortgage debt they secure is now 70%. In little over a decade, the went from handling $1 Trillion to 4$ Trillion dollars in mortgages. And, as I have stated in prior papers, though these two GSE's have no formal written backing by the U.S. Government, most feel the government would stand behind this debt. {This is why the Fannie Mae/Freddie Mac challenge is seen by many as parallel to the Savings/Loan scandal of the early 1990's. If, and I believe it will, when housing crashes, the government will stand behind this massive debt. That would mean the taxpayers (you and me) will pay the cost.}

Understand, the banks used to have a bit of control over housing prices. When one went to a bank to get a loan to make a purchase, the bank had to approve the loan. This meant an appraiser had to come and make his appraisal of the property. And they had to be close to 'right on'. No fudging here - the banks money, you know! But, when Freddie and Fannie said they would buy all the paper, heck, the banks just made a quick fund, then sold the paper. And today appraisers have no doubt come under pressure to be a bit liberal here and there. The result: less and less discipline on their part; and no doubt rules they have to follow - resulting in higher appraisals.

The last part of this challenge I will address is that during the past months, when corporations were being discovered to have 'cooked the books', by stating that their profits were higher than they really were, Freddie and Fannie were 'cooking their books' also! But, at the other end of the 'cooking process'. They actually hid how profitable they were! They were making so much money they were afraid that to let that information out. Afraid that it would cause a more volatile housing market and risk taking than their investors would like to see.

Once the housing market crashes, which no one doubts will happen soon, prices will ultimately have to go down. Discretionary income, becoming less and less due to stagnant income raises and job losses, will allow fewer to pay high prices for homes. Thus, prices will continue on a downward spiral, since the deflationary economy we are in will not cease to exist. Remember, Japan has been in a deflationary economy these past 12 years - and has witnessed property values drop as much as 50%. And, as property values decrease, then the tax base of each city/county will drop, thus bringing in less income to these entities, thus exasperating operating costs. Meaning more cuts - all over. And eventually, the city/county/state will have to find less expensive ways to provide services (does contracting out make sense?).

I hope you noted above where I stated that 'pension plans' were allowed to invest in properties, since they were now rated as 'low risk'. Now you understand how the pension plan problems that I see coming are tied to yet another problem; the housing downturn.

That 'transfer of wealth' statement seems more and more true to me. As the Information Age comes into full bloom, as the value of properties drops, those that own Millions of dollars of real estate today will own real estate worth less, and less. As the Information Age continues to mature, less and less work will be done in big concrete boxes, called offices. More will be done at home (see Frank Feather- Future Living.com). Those that work in the real estate industry will see their job classifications disappear - and they with them. No more real estate agents, mortgage agents. Cost too much. Easier way to do the same work - use the Internet!

Massive change is upon us. Those that understand the signs will prosper; those that do not - will not. Many will find they were a dinosaur - and hey, we need more oil anyway.

I close as I usually close by saying there is only ONE way that I see anyone living in the Land of Too Much Money: create massive residual income.

I attended a men's business forum last week and heard an amazing fact that I would like to share with you. It took Wal-Mart 12 years to get to $100 Million in sales; it took Amazon 4 years to get to $100 Million in sales; it took our Internet business model only 100 days to get to $100 Million in sales; and it took us only 31 days this past March to do $100 Million in sales!!! Is this pony running fast, or what??? Next, it will take 15 days to do $100 Million. Want a piece of this pie???????

Yours in building a Fantastic Future!

Ross

Chapter Four: April 2004
Week Three

Gooooooooood Evening, fellow Freedom Fighters!!!

Hope you all have had one prosperous week - and more in front of you. There are a whole lot of people out there that are seeking a more secure financial basis than they presently have - and all that stops them from finding it is if you do not share this business model with them. And some of these people can be found in the following articles:

1. Elk Grove job woes spotlighted (Sacto Bee; 04.15.04): Apple computer's elimination of 235 assembly plant jobs in Elk Grove this week.....

2. March prices jump sharply (Sacto Bee; 04.15.04): Consumer prices in March rose at some of the fastest rates in years, signaling a turning point in the economy that forecasts even higher prices for shoppers and higher interest rates for home buyers in coming months. Some say the FED could act as soon as summer and raise rates.

CONNECTING THE DOTS:

1. 235 more jobs eliminated, to be moved someplace else. And you just know that these folk that were 'pink slipped' cannot just uproot their families and move to wherever the jobs are headed. And what of jobs that head overseas? It was reported in the media over the past couple of days that both IBM and Citigroup have purchased outsourcing businesses

that are located in India! More and more jobs WILL be heading overseas; to people that speak and understand English very well, and simultaneously only need to be paid 20-25% of what the job pays here in the States. Every CEO of any large sized business that can take advantage of outsourcing will not have the luxury of deciding whether they want to do so - they know they HAVE to in order to keep profits (and dividends) as high as they can. Both candidates running for President will make statements to the effect that the will create new jobs - but isn't that really the job of businesses? Government should just make the playing field level for all who wish to play. And in the end, don't we all know that government really cannot create any meaningful jobs? So many who have, and will, lose their present positions will ultimately understand that the only way they can create some meaningful security is to be in charge of their own cash flow.

2. If the FED does indeed raise rates, we may well witness the beginning of the ultimate slowdown even before the elections! As I wrote in my Special Edition concerning the Real Estate industry, there is a crash coming - and it will be ushered in by higher interest rates. And when these rates become too high for the average person to qualify for a new home - then the beginning of this end will start. Couple that with rising costs of other essentials and monetary challenges for the average family will multiply. And of course, everyone is girding themselves for higher gasoline costs. If ever there was a time to be feverishly building your business, now is that time.

This is the week prior to our next business seminar weekend, and Linda and I will be there. And, we hope that each of you is able to find a way to attend too. Yes, it is not what one would call a 'cheap' event. But is it not true that there is cost for everything one does in life - as well as a cost for not doing it also? The question is which cost is higher? It would seem that a cost incurred upfront, though it might cause some discomfiture, is a smaller price to pay than long term 'not-enough-money-in-my-bank-account-itis'.

Well, all for now - and this weekend will be nothing short of STUPENDOUS!!!

Remember:

KNOWLEDGE IS POWER;
AND ONLY INFORMATION IF NOT USED

Ross

Chapter Four: April 2004
Week Four

Welcome home to all of you that attended the Seminar in LA this past weekend!

Hope all had an easy and uneventful return.

For those that could not make it - well, that you could not is the bad news; the good news is that the next business seminar comes up on July 30 - August 1, in Palm Springs. And the really exiting news is that Estela Salinas is going to be the featured speaker. Those that do not know her history - well, suffice to say this Lady is one of the few people that I would call 'hero'. That is if you would call one that puts themselves at risk (and I do mean harmful risk!) in order to succeed at fulfilling their mission! Anyway, Estela is one very goooood reason to put your making it a 'must do' - hearing her story will change the way you look at what you are doing, that is for sure!

Since I just returned home from our Seminar, I ask you to forgive the briefness of this edition. I have just one thought to pass on to you.

The Dow Jones.

In this month of April, the Dow started at 10375, and as of the 23rd was at 10473.

CONNECTING THE DOTS:

Each day between the 1st and the 23rd, the Dow hit various levels ranging from a low of 10310 (approximately) to a high of 10580 (again, approximately - I was reading off a bar graph). And, each day hundreds of millions of shares were bought and sold; some days I believe it was over a billion - if not for most days. So, for all of this selling and buying, who was involved? Well, of course we had some who sold, others who bought - and then the 'middle men'. I guess we call all these 'middle men' the stock "brokers". And each time stock is bought/sold - the one group who made money, regardless of what the stock eventually did, were all these "brokers". How many man hours were spent by how many people attempting to maximize their investments, to secure a stronger financial future? Too many to add up, I am sure. And what is the return for all these man hours? If one is to gauge the end result by the level of the Dow Jones, over 23 days, a plus 98. With what value?

Again, I would suggest that if one were to put just a portion of the man hours any one man put in during the past three weeks in attempting to make money on the stock market in building their Internet powered business, the time spent would return a greater value. This past weekend, in listening to many speakers and their stories and dreams for the future, one would come away knowing they are in the best business possible with. Great things are coming in the near future; and if you wish to witness the largest expansion the Internet will ever witness, then pack a lunch and watch. Better yet, become a part of it - and then enjoy the inevitable results of your labor!!!

Remember;

KNOWLEDGE IS POWER;
AND ONLY INFORMATION IF NEVER USED.

Ross

Chapter Five: May 2004
Special Edition

Well, here it is Monday, last day of the month - and life found me enjoying the last day of a three-day respite. Boy, did you need it as much as I did? At any rate, today we find an ongoing process that many are not comfortable with and that I have been wanting to address. Saturday, Lin and I went and saw 'Where Will You Be Tomorrow' - at least I think that is the name - a fictional piece concerning global warming and how it could affect the world. Regardless of your position on this issue, the main process (the melting of the Polar Icecap) generated in my mind a neat analogy to one of the challenges America finds to be most pressing: outsourcing. Thus, a Special Edition.

Consider that because of the ramifications of America prospering as it had during the Industrial Age, that America - and its work force, became the most prolific and powerful in the world; much like the Polar Ice Cap when compared with the level of the world's oceans. The Ice Pak stood head and shoulder above the oceans; the American worker and manufacturing stood head and shoulder above all other workers and countries. America became the dominant, most powerful country in the world. There was literally no country, nor work force, that could compete with America. America created on a scale that no other country could. America's working class was the envy of the world in the way it lived. But, as is always true in life, things change.

The movie I reference saw the Polar Ice melting - coming down in size, and simultaneously raising the level of the oceans. Heat was the 'action' that created this 'reaction'. Just recently Forrester Research stated that its forecast for the growth of the 'outsourcing' process was far off base; was in fact too low - outsourcing is occurring faster than even they saw it happening. The Internet is like the heat; it is melting the Ice Cap - which equates to jobs in America. All know that foreign workers are being paid 20% or so of what an American makes, for doing the same job. Yet, those outsourced jobs are paying people at a rate that they never had seen before. For once, their life style was rising! The Ice Cap melts, the ocean rises; overseas jobs are now paying more, American jobs less. The "paying field" is becoming more level. Some win, some lose.

The Information Age came into being due to the birth of the Internet - and a more level playing field for workers around the globe also came into existence. We will witness the death of the middle class in America, and simultaneously America will join the rest of the world, where there are only two classes: the class of 'too little money' and the class of 'too much money'. This is a non-reversible process. Outside America, individuals around the world will be able to make more money then ever before. Simultaneously, workers in America may well find themselves making less than they had been making, either as a function of inflation on goods/services and/or stagnant wages, or the actual lowering of wages. And the lowering of wages is already a proven process (the pilots for United Airlines took a 30% pay cut rather than see their business fold the tent and go out of business). One could say that most every job in America is vulnerable - one need only ask 'is this a job/process a computer program could do, or is this something a well educated individual in another country could do'? If there is even a small hint that the answer could be 'yes' - then do not be surprised to see it come to be.

• Education will no longer equate with great lifestyle, for a great education is available worldwide - and via the Internet! American jobs will continue to be lost, replaced in other countries. Jobs that today demand a large number of people to perform will start to lose numbers, using the Internet medium (Teachers at many levels will become at risk in the coming years). Businesses such as the Stock Market, Financial Planning, and Banking will change so much in the coming years that they will bear little resemblance to their present form. The 'Global Village' is emerging - those that prepare for it will benefit from the change. Those that ignore it will suffer the ramifications.

Like the Boy Scout motto states: Be Prepared

Ross

Chapter Five: May 2004

Well, here it is - the start of yet another new month.

I know you have set your goals for the next 30, whoops - 29 days - for a goal unset is a goal not hit. Of course, if your goal is to not hit any goal; well then, I guess you can hit your goal! Then one might ask: is that a goal worth achieving? Guess it gets down to where you want to get to. As Lewis Carroll stated in his Alice in Wonderland story, when the Cat asked Alice where she wanted to go, and Alice said she really did not know, the Cat replied "then any old road will do!"

As for roads that one might travel, let's check these out.

1. Retirees hit by benefits ruling (Sacto Bee; 04.23.04): The EEO (Equal Employment Opportunity Commission) voted to allow employers to reduce or eliminate company-paid health benefits for retirees when they become eligible for Medicare at age 65.

2. Changes push Dow away from 'industrial' (Sacto Bee; 05.02.05): For the first time in four years, the Dow Jones industrial average is losing some of its 30 component companies and gaining some others. Asked to come in were insurance giant AIG, Pfizer (pharmaceuticals) and Verizon (communication). Asked to leave were AT&T, International Paper and Eastman Kodak.

3. Sorry, lost the article - saw it in the Sacto Bee this past week: Milk prices will shoot up from around $2.50 a gallon

or so to close to $3.90 a gallon (it depends on where one buys it). But, the price is definitely going up - way up.

CONNECTING THE DOTS:

1. One might say ' so what ' - retirees get to get on Medicare at 65 anyway. But, ask more retirees and they are not too happy about this change. So, who wins, who loses? Who wins are the companies that will no longer have to pay for health benefits for their retirees - they can now use that money for other things (like increasing their bottom line?) Who loses will be the Medicare system and/or the individuals themselves. Will the Medicare system, already spending Billion and Billions, have enough money to do the 'right thing' for all these people? And, will these retirees actually receive less in medical benefits than they need? As is always the truth - it just gets down to money.

2. So what is really happening here? Just one more example of how the world is quickly leaving the Industrial Age and shifting into the Information Age. This change pushes the Dow more into a global direction - and also indicates which group is more important to the U.S. economy. The market value of the three firms pushed out are about $43 Billion, while the incoming group represents some $566 Billion. Annual revenues for the now 'geriatric set' were some $73 Billion, while the youngsters were at $194 Billion! And remember, the Dow is meant to reflect the U.S. stock market. Watch for more changes in firms sent to the 'farm' - and the new kids coming in! Truly, the Information Age is blossoming as we watch. Do what you have to do so that your life is more like a Rose than a Geranium!

3. Milk - got some? Well, I love iced milk during the Summer (and the other Seasons too) - so guess I had just better find a way to not let a measly $1.00 a gallon slow my drink-

ing habit down. With fewer diary cows and higher feed costs, do you think the cost of milk will go down?

As a 'wrap up' - do you think that gasoline (going up and up) and now milk (going up and up) are reflected in any way in the 'number' our government issues as a "cost of living" change? Yet, if it costs more money for stuff we need and do buy "anyway", and by definition costs going up can be called 'inflation' - just because it is not calculated as 'inflation' - is it anyway? Remember the Bard said " A rose by any other name is a rose indeed ". (You know the Bard - Shakespeare!).

In conclusion, if milk, gasoline, housing and vehicles - whose costs continue to spiral up - do not constitute inflation - yet each and everyone of us wishes or needs them, how can we most easily earn the money to have them? Oh yes - the answer is in the wind! In fact, part of it was on the airwaves this morning - where Nutrilite presented a one-hour program on health. Linda and I watched it - and it was EXCELLENT!!!

If you have to do something 'anyway'; and you will spend some money on it 'anyway', and you need some basic items of life 'anyway', does it make sense to just go out and spend your hard earned money to profit another, or does it make more sense to spend all this 'anyway' money in YOUR store and make some more money for you - ANYWAY???

Remember,

KNOWLEDGE IS POWER;
IF NOT USED IT IS ONLY INFORMATION.

See you on the HiWays and the BiWays.

Ross

Chapter Five: May 2004
Week Two

A most Happy Mothers day to all you Mothers out there - and to those that are reading this missive - a Happy Mothers day to your Mother also! My mother is no longer with me - but the things she did in raising me have not, nor will they, be forgotten. Mothers are very Special People - and they should be acknowledged as such each day of one's life - not just on one day a year.

That which you do and speak can acknowledge this Special-ness.

So, what news came out this past week?

1. Influx of foreign workers lowers wages, study say (Sacto Bee; 05.04.04): Two decades growth in the supply of immigrant workers cost native-born American men an average of $1700 in annual wages by 2000. Congressional Democrats and Republicans have both launched legislation that would allow an increased flow of immigrants. In the report showing this lowering of wages, it was suggested that the effect of these proposals by legislators would be to depress wage growth for Americans at ALL (capitalization by me) levels of education.

CONNECTING THE DOTS:

1. Immigration is with us, and not much will change with respect to that during the coming months and years. Whether this immigration is legal or illegal, the change (or rather the lack

of change) in wage growth will be part of life. And notice that the level of education does not change this fact either! Let this article allow me to segue into my next thought.

Last Thursday at the Holiday Inn, where Charlie Hunt presented our business model, Charlie also presented some facts forwarded to him by Karen Waddell. Karen shared with Charlie the findings of a PhD, out of Taiwan. The findings this PhD presented in a paper, summarized, is this: work until you are about 50, and then retire and have a life expectancy of about 79 or so. Work until you are 65, and then retire and have a life expectancy of about 67!!! Well, which seems better to you? To quote Leif Johnson, the long-retired ophthalmologist: " 1, or 2?" Given that you are reading and taking this one question test, I believe I am substantially correct in stating that ALL of you chose "1" - would you agree? Given this, which path in life will allow you to get to "1"?

Society today preaches ' go to school, get a good education, work hard for thirty (or forty) years, and then retire into the Golden Years.' Many who start higher education (after high school) never finish. Does this imply that higher education was a poor choice? NO! It implies that they made the choice to not finish. All who go to school pay for each unit of class taken; some say an inordinate amount per unit. All will then pay additional monies for books required for the class. Today it is not unlikely that one book can cost $150.00. Does this book cost imply someone is gaining at their expenditure? YES! Those who are sharing the information contained in those books are only being paid for their knowledge. If one learns well what is taught in their books, cannot they then go on to write a 'better' book, and thus gain financially for their work? YES! Those who are able to maintain this discipline for four or more years than matriculate (graduate). Does the degree earned guarantee a great paying job, or even one with any security for life? NO! And, does the prospect of working and paying all the $ums required for a higher education, exhibited via a 'Degree', seem worth the result of working for 30 or 40 years? That answer has to be your own. But, before answering, review the information regarding age of retirement and balance of life expectancies above.

What you have before you, since you are reading this, is the chance to take part in yet a different type of education. Higher education to be sure - but of a different type. The "professors" that we have the chance to take classes from, unlike so many of those in traditional education, have actually done what they teach! Who better to learn from: one that has done, or one that has only learned how a thing is done? And should education be totally free? Or is there value in learning that which can give you your hearts desire? And if there is value, is it not worth making a sacrifice for?

Does it make sense if I were to say that the traditional educational system "brain washes" all of us? Not in the negative sense of brain-washing, but in the sense of creating a non-chaotic society that has common values? For in the beginning (not THAT far back!) as Mac teaches, there was fruitfulness in the process of being more educated, having a better job, and living better. But do not times change? And as Mac also teaches, the job is not capable of doing what it once did. Thus, people seek answers in different places. Such as starting their own businesses.

You have all heard, or read, that 95% of all businesses started do not last one year. Does this mean that there is something wrong with starting a business? Heck NO! It was all about the dream of an individual. And that s/he did not have all necessary tools required for success in that particular endeavor. But again, does just starting a business imply success? From personal experience, backed with ten years of college and three degrees, I say: NO! In one business I started and owned, I was successful (that means made decent to great money) for almost 30 years, until I closed it down. Another lasted 3 years and was short of successful (actually, very short!). The difference? In one I had mentors to learn from (guess which one) - the other I did not.

What I have come to understand through the teachings of Robert Kiyosaki is this: whichever business model one wishes to become successful in, one MUST become educated in thinking as that model demands. The question each of us faces when we make the decision to do follow a business model is this: do I use the thinking processes already taught to me that are only applicable in the 'A' System, or do I accept and accrue the thinking processes demanded for success in 'B'System ? This is analogous to asking ones self if I already speak French well, is it good enough to become successful in a place where only Spanish is spoken? Again, you must answer for yourself. Know only that education is not for free; for anything worth knowing takes education - and there is always a price to be paid. Life teaches us that education is never free. Formal, or informal, one pays a price for education. Failing to gain any education at all - well, one still pays a price. The price of living not as well as was possible. Either way, each of us will pay a price. Which price you are willing to pay will be determined by you.

Inasmuch as it is Mothers Day, and Linda is a Mother, I am finished with this week's issue. She is someone very Special in my life - and the lives of our two children.

Remember:

KNOWLEDGE IS POWER;
IF NOT USED IT IS ONLY INFORMATION.

See you on the HiWays and the BiWays!!!

Ross

Chapter Five: May 2004
Week Three

Howdy on a nice Sunny Sunday!!!

Weather is fantastic here in Elk Grove - not too cool, not too hot - just right. And, the Kings are on in the next hour so I thought I better get this edition out while in a 'good' mood - 'cause I might be a bit unhappy later in the day!!! For those Laker fans out there - well, I really have no doubt we will be seeing your guys soon!!!

So, what have headlines have we seen this past week?

1. Cities are big losers in plan by governor (Sacto Bee; 05.16.04): Elk Grove stands to lose $1 million over the next two fiscal years under Governors plan to cut state funding to cities, counties and special service districts.

2. Inflation gains steam (Sacto Bee, 05.16.04): Consumer prices crept up in April...but the report also suggested that inflation had probably accelerated in May. In any case, the rise in inflation over the past four months has lasted long enough to convince many economists that the Fed must soon raise interest rates.

3. Earn rebates towards any car with any purchase (Ad in Parade - insert in Sacto Bee, 05.16.04): 5% rebates until .6.01.05.

4. Purchase Direct TV and get free Tivo (Advertising on television): Purchase - actually get free, up to four lines of Satellite TV and get Free TIVO with it.

CONNECTING THE DOTS:

1. Question: who populates these cities and counties? Last I heard, it was people like you and me. So, how does funding cuts change our lives? Well, last I read the County of Sacrament was trying to determine what accounts to cut - which means what people lose services? And, additionally, who will lose jobs? The biggest challenge to this action is that the State, which had always passed this money on to the cities/ counties (surely there must be a law that mandates this; anyone out there know for sure?) decides that since it is broke, that it makes sense to take someone else's money to pay its bills. The "up" side of this is that the Governor is also proposing to put a law on the books to make sure this does not happen again. This is like a burglar stealing your hard earned money, but saying he will then prohibit himself from ever again robbing you! Boy, that would sure make a guy (or a gal too!) feel really good about the robbery, huh? Lose money that is truly yours, get a promise that it will not happen again, and then you get to figure out how to pay your bills with zilch in the bank account. Guess it might make sense to have more money than you need to live on so that when unexpected things happen to you, you really do not get affected. Surely there must be some way this could happen?

2. Ah, our good friend 'inflation'! I say 'good friend' since Alan Greenspan has been heard, and reported to say, that a little inflation is good for us! But, rising interest rates will have a contrary effect upon the stock market - and the housing market too! And this 'little bit of inflation' has NOT had the rising cost of gasoline and milk factored into the equation! Guess that the rising cost of these two items are not really an

indication of inflation - but we pay as if they were anyway. As a sidebar, I saw it written the other day that Greenspan stated that this 'little bit of inflation would enable factories to raise their pricing a bit; but also it was reported in last weeks Money Talk edition that wages are stagnant - and will probably stay that way (the State is not considering any pay increases for its employees this year either!). So, prices go up, wages stay stagnant; will more stuff get bought, or less?

3. Jeepers, credit cards giving "Benefit" to those that use their cards!!! Making an investment, and receiving a return on that investment, for money one will spend "ANYWAY"!!! What a concept!!! Wouldn't that be nice if it happened in more places????

4. TIVO!!! How many of you just LOVE to get that acting stuff out of the way so that you can watch one more mind expanding TV AD??? Well, with TIVO, you can eliminate ALL advertising - well, for those that hate ads. What might happen if TIVO is used by only some 40% of the population? How many ads will never be seen? And, how do networks make their money? Maybe via ADS??? And, if no one is watching ADS, will a ',manufacturer/middleman' see any value in spending millions of dollars to show ads that close to half the population will never watch? So, what might many of these producers/movers of goods do then? Maybe find a business model that will give BENEFIT to those that buy and use their product? Know any business model that can do this? A business model IN PLACE that is already proven in the market place? If so, better get ready for a fast, fun ride!

The commentary on items 3. and 4. are obviously my own, and are very biased thoughts. All of us are a part of a movement that has no other conclusion than businesses will survive only when they ultimately realize that giving the consumer a benefit to use their product will ensure their continued existence. Advertising, as was created during the Industrial Age, is on its way out - with over 300 channels available for the consumer to plug into. Add to that the disdain of most of the public as to watching advertising - well, you get the drift. Remember the short time that movie houses actually showed advertising before the previews came on? That did not last long as they no doubt received some serious backlash from the ticket buying public. With TIVO on the horizon, the business model that we are all a part of will become the dominant process of moving product.

Here is to evolution (business-wise, that is)!!! We are all in the right place at the right time doing the right thing with the right business.

Remember:

KNOWLEDGE IS POWER;
IF NOT USED IT REMAINS ONLY INFORMATION

Be the last one on your block to turn the porch light off!

Ross

Chapter Five: May 2004
Week Four

What a fantastic day today was - Spring is definitely here - and that means that Summer is not too far behind. And, next week is a three-day weekend - so I know you will have something planned for a really good time. Talking about a "good time" - I just have to share a word about last nights 'get-together' at the home of Charlie and Christy. Now, most of us have been to other 'nuts-n-bolts' (teaching and training for those that might be new to our business model) - and they are always informative and enjoyable - BUT: last night was so far out in front of any we have attended (and there have been many that we have attended) that it cannot be measured! I mean, the two hours flew by so fast; each of the speakers not only shared their thoughts - but it was just "fun" too. Rick Bray, who came to his first ever in our group, said after ward that he had never been to a Nuts'nBolts that was this much fun - and also where he learned as much as he did. Rick also said he would invite his new partners to the next one "to just have a bunch of fun; and heck, they could not help but learn stuff anyway." Ask anyone you know who was there - they will give you the skinny. And know one thing: this is just the FIRST of many that will be just as much fun - so make sure you do NOT miss any others. And the kudos have to go to Charlie and Christy, who set the tone for what we do and how we do it. Way to go guys! We are so proud to be associated with people of your ilk.

Ok, now to the news that doesn't sound like news:

1.   More check out Internet groceries (Sacto Bee; 04.23.04): After the spectacular crashes of big-name Internet grocers in the late 1990's, the dream of a grand new wave of online food stores appeared to fizzle. But, with meager fanfare, grocers have made the Internet shopping available to tens of millions of consumers nationwide. Now, it is no longer a question of whether they can be successful, but rather of how big they will become.

2. Governor still short of balancing state budget (Sacto Bee; 04.18.04): The revised budget of Gov. Arnold S. as proposed last week on paper appears to balance the budget. But, without an economic boom that no one is expecting, Gov. A's budget is still out of balance between tax receipts and spending. The structural gap they say will be eliminated in 2005-06 - but cannot show how that will happen.

3. Stocks tumble around world (Sacto Bee; 04.18.04): A killing in Iraq, surging oil prices and uncertainty in India shake up investors; Dow hits low for year.

CONNECTING THE DOTS:

1. Ah, yeah - remember Webvan? Webvan was cited by Frank Feather (the noted Futurist) in his first book (Future-Consumer.com) as being one of the five businesses that would be the biggest in future years. What did it in? From what I have learned - it was just too successful! And also a bit in front of the future. Today, Safeway is doing tons of Internet business - and has yet to advertise its presence! Peapod, a name many of you will remember, is still in business in a big way, and expects to reach some 14 million households by 2006. People ARE going to continue to use this service, and the numbers will increase. Why? Is it not true that the number one commodity that people want more of and have less of is: T-I-M-E??? The only question I see is when will one of these

growing grocery online businesses create a partnership with a known Internet distribution business? Then, who will you buy YOUR groceries from??? Oh heck, I know. You guys have all read HouseHold Gold - so you will buy from YOURSELF!!! Whata concept!!!!! And, how soon until one of the major oil companies tie in with us? Talk about creating a monopoly - buy giving, rather than just taking! The future is changing fast, and we all are so in the right position. (Oh, and the other 4 picks by Feather are still alive and well.)

2. This 'structural gap' sure seems to be a nice phrase, since we hear it all the time. But, what it means is this: they spend more then they get. What happens when you spend more money than you make in a month? Do you call it a 'Structural Gap', or just that you have a case of 'more month than money' woes? Call it whatever you want, it still means the same thing. Economic challenges in the future. Either spend less now, get the credit cards paid, or maybe go BK. With the State, it will no doubt mean that more employees will not get a raise this year (that means that with inflation they will make less money this year than last, all the while cost continue to go up). Also, that many will be asked to take another 5% pay cut (of course, the ones at the top make more than others, so they don't need it as much anyway). But, if most people live to their income, doesn't that mean they will suffer too? Watch as more programs get cut, costs for residents in varying fields go up (check out the new rates for college education), and people get laid off.

3. This type of occurrence continues to confirm in my mind that there really are no real leaders in the economic arena out there today. Maybe the one 'leader' would be Alan Greenspan; or maybe even just below him might be Warren Buffett - but people listen when Greenspan hic-cups even; not so with Buffett. It appears that no one really has any handle on what is going on, or what to do. Greenspan has been re-

nominated by President Bush to head the Fed, and Alan said 'sure, why not?' Might it be that President Bush has done so, knowing that the whole world knows how Greenspan has accomplished much during his past 17 years in the Fed, and thus those advising this action will make everyone feel that the President has the economy in mind and is doing the 'right thing'. So, in one light it would seem to be the proper political action. Greenspan lived and learned, and quite well, Industrial Age economics - yet we are now in the early stages of Information Age economics - which I don't think anyone really knows the bottom line to. And you know from previous papers that I feel history shows that each new Age ushers in its own set of economic rules, where the rules of the past Age either disappear completely, or end up being footnotes. And, could it be that Alan Greenspan, now some 77 years of age, accepts this position once more in order to maintain his position of relevance? For once he retires, his relevance retires with him - and he is out of the limelight. Given that you or I were in his shoes, might we not do the same?

Change is coming, that no one doubts. Trading time for money (again, an Industrial Age concept) will cease to create for the employee the ability to live well and prepare for retirement. Retirement (another Industrial Age creation) will fade away as a concept that only seems to work for some (that some will be the some that have created residual income, while they did have a job). Assets will not create wealth; cash flow creates wealth. With cash flow one can accumulate assets - but with the ease of not having to have those assets create cash flow (does your home, really a liability - but the equity could be called an asset- create any cash flow to you?). What's a Guy, or Gal, or a Guy and a Gal, do these days? For all I have learned, only one thing to do: find some way to create unlimited cash flow. Each of you has the capacity to do so; what each of you must do is to look within yourself and know that there IS a "seed of greatness" in there. Then, find a

"Farmer" (we call them Mentors) who will assist your "seed of Greatness" to grow and prosper. Do not fear change; embrace change! Your life WILL change, your future WILL change, as you WILL change. Don't walk; don't skip; don't jog; but RUN away from Mediocrity - straight into YOUR future, as a changed person. A person who will then find that they have become the "Farmer", and then assist the next generation of Greatness.

My Friends, resolve to become the best Farmer you can - and you will.

No Greater Love is that than when one will lay down his life to help another. "Farmers" give their lives to their seeds. Plant some, raise some.

Yours in planting seeds,

Ross

Whoops:

Remember:

KNOWLEDGE IS POWER;
IF NOT USED, IT IS ONLY INFORMATION

Chapter Five: May 2004
Week Five

Hello All -

and I hope you are having an enjoyable Memorial Holiday weekend.

Most of all, I hope that each of us is taking a moment to understand as fully as we might what this weekend truly represents. As much as those of us who still work enjoy the three-day weekend, this Holiday is not about us; it is about others that gave of themselves - to others that they would never know. And gave in the fullest that any can give. We live in a land of utmost opportunity, a land that we who live in should realize has been truly blessed. What we think of this blessing is no doubt best expressed in what we give back.

A challenge that faces each of us is in the value of the "coin" of the written/spoken word. Words 'mean' things, and I would share that the use of any word has as much value as in the value of a 'bill' that we spend on any item (ten dollar bill, etc). Too often we use words as valueless coin - something to be tossed around in conversation, conveying a thought, but not a meaning. Again, words 'mean things'. A thought might be an idea, but a 'meaning' has depth. A word that came to me this morning is 'Amen'; probably most used, maybe only used, in a church or prayer setting. Yet, do many know its meaning? In Hebrew, it means 'let it be'. Not a thought, a 'meaning' - LET IT BE! We use the word 'job' extensively, yet do we know what it 'means' in this Age? Webster declares that a 'job' is "to deal in as a middleman". (On a humorous note, it is also defined "to seek private gain under pretense of public service." Could Webster have realized what many Politicians really do?). And do we not witness today the continuing elimination of the 'middleman'? Would it then follow that what we are witnessing in the elimination of the 'middlemen' in distribution would also be true for all? For does not anyone in most any 'job' act as a middleman, even in the processing of information? Maybe we will soon see yet another definition in Webster's Dictionary for 'job': just over broke.

Segueing from 'broke' into today's news:

1. Teacher pension fund will fall billions short (Sacto Bee; 05.28.04): After a string of stock market losses and sub par investment returns, the Calif. State Teachers Retirement System must pour in an additional $1 Billion in the coming years to ensure the fund can pay benefits over the long haul. Cash-strapped school districts, the state and teachers must increase their contributions. "We were surprised by the magnitude. We have to have an increase in contributions. The liability is only going to get bigger the longer we go on without resolution", said Sherry Reser, a spokeswoman for CalSTRS, the nations third largest public pension fund.

2. Are Boomers Maturing? (Wall Street Journal; 05.30.04): Will baby boomers have a comfortable retirement, or will their spending habits do them in? There is evidence that a more than 77 Million strong generation is becoming more conservative in its retirement outlook. A study in 1998 showed that 80% of boomers planned on spending their retirement years 'working'! The same number shown in a 2003 study. Most categories showed work for part-time, start their own business, etc; only 20% felt they would not work at all.

CONNECTING THE DOTS:

1. If you know anyone who is a teacher, you might ask them if CalSTRS alerted them to this fact yet. No doubt most will only find out that a challenge exists in their fund when they find their contributions are scheduled to go up - without any wage increase, of course! (State cannot afford wage increase, so districts cannot afford one either!) The number of public plans with shortfalls will increase to 75% this year, up from 31% two years ago. Of course, many teachers will reply with the verbiage of "our pension is guaranteed by law", which is true. The pension may be guaranteed, but no doubt at a fixed rate. Of course, they might then say that they get 'cost of living' (COLA's) raises; but ask one who IS retired how that 1.7% increase helped them live any better - when we witness costs across the board going up many percentage points each year. The average retirement check for a teacher is $3676 a month - yet with an average 6% inflation each year, if a teacher retired today, that $3676 would be worth only $1838 in buying power in twelve years!!! How well will they live with that amount? And, saying that, lets segue into point number 2.

2. Yup, they sure are! America is getting grayer (some might even point at me to prove that point!) I guess that the only thought I have to share on this topic is this: anyone who feels 'really comfortable with their pension plan - is probably the one that most needs to be a bit afraid - maybe, a lot afraid. If public pension plans come up short, and public entities have to find the money, who will they come to? Your house and mine, in the form of taxation. But, ultimately, even the politician knows there is just so much blood they can suck out of any turnip. And if private pension plans are having the same challenge (and those have already been so noted in prior columns), who pays for them? And if no one has the money to pay for them, what quality of life will they have? And ulti-

mately, will it not be a 'hue and cry' that 'they deserve a better end' - and 'why didn't someone see this coming'?

Well, many of us DO see it coming - and in the end we are all responsible for our decisions. Each of us will live as we will in the future based upon the decisions we make in the todays. Come to an understanding of what the Information Age is truly about - and with your understanding, make the changes in what you do and how you do it so that you will be able to live as you truly desire to live - not as you have to.

Concluding thought: This past weekend Linda and I had the opportunity to 'break bread' with a couple that we are coming to know very well. During the many topics of conversation it came to me that, thanks to all of you for accepting Money Talk, that I have come to better understand who and what I am all about. My thoughts come as I write; most times only as a response to an article or statement. I wish not to convert anyone to my way of thinking, for I live in 'my world', shaped by all I have come to learn and understand. What I truly wish is for each of you to come to your own personal understanding of the 'world you live in', and then act accordingly. But, when you have discovered 'your world' - I pray that the words you use in setting your course of action, you will use with value and true 'meaning'.

Let your 'yes' mean 'YES' !

Find your 'seeds' - invest your life in them, and become Significant.

Remember:

KNOWLEDGE IS POWER;
IF NOT USED, ONLY INFORMATION.

Yours for a Fantastic Tomorrow for ALL!!!

Farmer Ross

Chapter Six: June 2004
Week One

Last month of the first half of the year!

Wow!!! Time flies, does it not? And how are each of you doing in hitting the goals you set for yourself 60 days ago? Good news is that you still have 30 more days in which to hit them - so lets see the fur fly!

Talking about fur, last night 'fur' sure was a blast! And I have to be talking about the Seminar at which Michael and Lynette Singleton were the featured speakers. Talk about the 'heavy hitters' being there, Charlie and Christy - Larry and Patty - Bill and Michele were there, as were a great number of others. In fact, the place was totally packed. Michael talked about how our business model is attracting an even younger set of people and how we may see some changes that reflect this change. At any rate, you needed to be there to get the gist of his thoughts - and Michael has some pretty deep thoughts - he did not get to early retirement sitting on a stool. So, get your calendar set for the next Seminar and make it a point to be there.

Now, on to what I found to be a very interesting column item.

1. Undisputed King of the Casino (Sacto Bee; 06.06.04); nearly 40 million Americans played a slot machine in 2003. Every day in the U.S., slot machines take in, on average, more than $1 Billion in wagers. All told, North American casi-

nos took in $30 Billion from slots in 2003 - an amount that dwarfs the $9 Billion in tickets sold in North America for movie theaters that year. Craps, blackjack and roulette once defined organized gambling - but has been replaced by slot machines at the business that drives the industry today. Some see this action as the 'dumbing down' of American life. Playing craps, or blackjack, means knowing and understanding a complex set of rules. With slots, no thinking is required.

CONNECTING THE DOTS:

1. You might think this is a strange column for me to use, yet I see it as another proof of the changing of American society. One casino sees this growth in slot machine playing as indicative of a growing laziness in the educational system. Or, maybe we have just become intellectually lazy. When one elderly man was asked why he play slots, he replied, "I don't have to think."

A friend of mine who has been involved in the construction industry for some time made a comparable statement to me when we were discussing the lack of knowledgeable workers in the 'trades'. He made the comment that the industry was just 'dumbing down' the building process. And know what? He is correct. In the old days, a carpenter built a home from the foundation up. Today, especially in the subdivision construction arena, there are 'framers' - who just frame the walls; 'joisters' - who lay trusses and floor systems, 'siders' - who just apply siding; and a whole bunch more 'components'. In plumbing, where for decades water flowed through copper pipe - which mandated one who knew how to 'sweat' pipe and such, water lines are now plastic - with copper only coming through the sheetrock! Yes, we are headed toward a society where less and less knowledge of a subject is required, with many needed to just do what one used to do. But, with the 'dumbing down' process, would it not seem true that since an individual knew less, then s/he could be paid less? Couple this dumbing down process found in the construction industry with the amazing growth seen in the gambling industry, and what might that say? Are people just hoping to win that one 'BIG ONE' - so that life gets better for them for the rest of their life? You who are involved with this business model see the writing on the wall, and are to be commended for seeing it! As I believe Michael said last night, build this business, and you WILL pay a price to build it; don't build it and you WILL pay a price for not building it - but, pay a price we each will. So, does it make more sense to pay a price one time and live well for the rest of your life, or to pay the price for the rest of your life and never live well? Each of us chooses.

As that Knight in Indiana Jones and the Holy Grail once said, " choose well!"

All for now, talk to you next week. Until then, remember:

KNOWLEDGE IS POWER;
AND IF NOT USED, IT IS JUST INFORMATION.

Find a "seed', nurture the "seed", and become Significant!

Farmer Ross

Chapter Six: June 2004

Week Two

Greetings to all of you - I hope you are having a most enjoyable Sunday!

This morning I was coming back from breakfast and drove through old Land Park. Many of you might not know the Land Park area of Sacramento, but it is where the Zoo is, and also a small golf course. Watching some of them play as I went by, it came to me that Golf is much like this business. We all "tee off" - meaning we get started, and have a goal in sight - that little hole on the "green". To get there we use a variety of clubs, depending upon the lie of the ball. Just as we use our people skills in varying manner due to the "lie" of the thoughts/beliefs of the person we are sharing this business model with. Sometimes we use just a few "clubs", meaning a quick trip to the "hole". Sometimes the ball goes in directions we definitely did not want it to go - but go after it we do. Ultimately, we wish to "hole out" - and then start on another new "hole". Maybe we all really are playing golf and just never realized it!

Now, for all you golfers out there - those that really are and those that might not realize they are - the following news of the week:

1. Optimism on the jobs front in short supply (Sacto Bee; 06.07.04): Results of the interviews of some 1009 women and 997 men show that women are more skeptical about finding a 'good' job than men. Some 74% of women are in this group,

while only 66% of the men are. One of the findings indicates how employers of low-wage workers, responding to economic pressure, are reducing costs: freezing of wages, cuts in benefits, increase of workload, subcontract, temps, automation - and what is particularly devastating - outsourcing.

2. Public-pension flap mirrors state's chronic budget crisis (Sacto Bee; 06.11.04): A few years ago... Davis and legislators were spending their way into a horrendous budget crisis and simultaneously sowing seeds for a monumental problem in financing pensions for public employees. The most spectacular was a 50% boost for Highway Patrol Officers. CalPERS anticipated state contributions to remain below the 1998-99 numbers for the next decade. Wrong. Stock market slides, PERS looses billions of dollars, pension costs shoot up. Arnold uses borrowed money and waits for a rising economy to balance the budget, rather than raise taxes. (A synopsis of the column)

3. Greenspan wars on rates (Sacto Bee; 06.09.04): Fed Chairman Alan Greenspan said Tuesday that the central bank will raise interest rates as aggressively as necessary to keep inflation in control.

4. Truckers from Mexico now in USA (Sacto Bee; title is mine, sorry - could not find the article but need to comment on it); The Supreme Court of the USA ruled and now truckers are now able to run into the USA, due to NAFTA.

CONNECTING THE DOTS:

1. I doubt that any of you would question the poll result that optimism for finding a 'good job' is this low. Do any of you know of someone who lost his/her job during the past year and has found a new job equal to it? And just what is a 'low wage worker' today? Have you ever thought of just what it takes

to get through an average month with one or two kids? Could you make it on a 'take home' pay of $2000/month? House payment, food, insurance, gas, clothing (as required) - can it be done on $500 a week? And if you take home $2000, then you probably have to be making something like $3000/month (before withholding). That is $36,000/year. With no pay raises (see a teacher for this one!), cuts in benefits (or you pay more for benefits). It is not to hard to feel why an average of 70% of respondents to this query feel there is no longer a 'good job'.

2. A continuing saga. I understand that PERS is now only receiving some 92% of what it needs to pay its bills (from its investments) and STRS only 86%. Either employees pay more, or get less, or the public entity they work for pays more, which comes only from taxes (so do they go up?). And, as for retiree's, they are caught in the middle. Arnolds hope for a rising economy may stay just that: a hope. The construction industry has long been the 'driver' of the American economy; when construction is at its highest, purchases of manufactured goods (think stoves, microwaves, lights, etc) that are necessary to be installed in a new home fuel industry upon industry. Yet, the housing crash is an inevitable occurrence that almost all knowledgeable individuals know will happen. When that occurs, how then to fund all the retirement needs? Maybe only through the downsizing of State employment, curtailment of State services (more lost jobs?), and the raising of taxes (can the average person afford to pay more than they do today?). Time will tell.

3. Well, if Alan raises interest rates to contain inflation (what? I keep hearing that inflation is only at 2% or so), the mortgage rates would also rise, yes? And if they continue to go up, would fewer people be able to qualify for a mortgage? And if fewer people can qualify, would sales drop? And if they drop, could prices start to go down? And if they go down, and down, to a point where more can qualify for a mortgage, then

what of the value of all those homes that were purchased at a much higher price? Would they lose value? And continue to do so? And if wages are as stagnant as most all know, then would these new prices on previously bought homes have to stay down? And maybe below the amount of the mortgage? And then what? Oh, the fact that gas continues to go up (guess that is not in the inflationary index), and medical costs go up (neither is that I think - in the index), and food goes up (whoa - that sure ain't in the index!), but none of that is inflation - but wages do not go up - how well does the average individual live?

4. This one I just HAD to comment on. We have all heard and realize that 'outsourcing' is a fact of life that will continue, and continue to grow in numbers of jobs sent overseas. But, is it not the case that most of us would think of 'outsourcing' as "jobs being done by people in a different country for less money" - like those that make basketball shoes, or those that do work sent over and done on computers? WHOA!!! Could it not be the case that all the truck drivers from Mexico are also 'outsourcing' the jobs of American truck drivers? Diesel cost is like $1.60/gallon in Mexico; almost $2.30/gallon in California. Drivers in California (and probably in the USA) make about $20-25/hour - do you think drivers from Mexico make that much? Or more like $5-10/hour? One of the trucker's association board members who owns a trucking firm even said that he would probably have some 30% of his trucking done by these new drivers/firms. So, given this fact, might all of us take a hard look down the road of the future and see how just possibly someone else might do our job - and for less money?

Gonna close on the happenings of this past week: the end of the Reagan Era. Nothing political, just about the man. Was listening to Tom Sullivan the other day and he posed the question of why so much outpouring from the country? This 'outpouring' was more than anyone had ever thought would happen. I had to think about it, since I too felt a loss. Why? For me, it was because though I might not have agreed with all his positions, he had Character and Integrity. In the Today paper (06.11.04), I post "Leadership lessons from the Reagan years":

1. Start with a moral foundation. Reagan saw right and wrong.

2. The vision thing matters. Reagan had long-term visions to the end.

3. Take the heat. Make tough calls - and stick with them.

4. Be comfortable in your own skin. Leaders who are at home in their own skin give the OK for others to feel at home in theirs.

5. Maintain a sense of humor. At all times.

6. Be a Great Communicator. Leaders need to show emotion and passion. Where it comes to vision and strategy, "say it well, say it often, say it simply and say it passionately."

7. Delegate. Get out of the way of talented people.

Hey guys and gals, hope this makes some sense to you.

Find your dream, give of yourselves - help other 'seeds' to become all they can be.

Remember:

KNOWLEDGE IS POWER;
IF NOT USED, IT IS ONLY INFORMATION.

Yours in Dreaming and Farming,

Ross

Chapter Six: June 2004
Week Three

To all you Fathers out there, a HAPPY FATHERS DAY to you!!! And even if you are not one, then a HAPPY FA-THERS DAY to your father too. My father is no longer with me, but I think of him - especially during this day. Funny how stuff your father shared (well, we took it as being 'told') with us makes so much more sense later on in our life than it did when we first heard it. And also, in the remembering of some of these things that he shared with us, we can now see how things are continually changing in our lifetimes, giving more veracity to the old saying "Change is the only constant in life." That may sound like an oxymoron, and probably fits the definition pretty well - but it would also appear to be sooooo true. And with the premise of things changing over time, that is my segue into the first, and only article that I will share this day:

1. Mortgage gamble (Sacto Bee; 06.14.04): Despite in-creasing prices and waning affordability, the housing market has gained surprising momentum this year. The market's en-durance is widely attributed NOT (caps by me) to the tra-ditional fuels for record sales - strong job growth and wage hikes - but to low interest rates, increased use of adjustable-rate mortgages, relaxed lending rules and a string of innova-tions such as zero-down home loans. Today, another breed of a relatively risky mortgage is helping propel the market: "interest only loans."

CONNECTING THE DOTS:

1. Do any of you remember (well, if you are not at least 40, then you probably do not) when one purchased a new car - and the normal life of the loan was 36 months? I do - and many others do also. Then, the loans went to 48 months, 60, then 72 and even 84! Hey, seven or eight years to pay for a car! Then, came low interest rates, then lower interest rates (going down to zero interest!), then cash back, and cash back with zero interest rates. Also, in what I call the 'old days', when one went to purchase a new car the salesman would ask one question: "how much do you want to pay?" What do they ask today? They ask: " what amount do you want your payment to be?" The cost is not the issue, rather the monthly payment. Why? Might it be that the issue is not what to pay in total, rather how much one can pay monthly? And then the question comes up, why that? Might that answer be a 'continued lack of discipline' regarding delayed gratification? And one more question: Why were all these different packages for purchase created (other than the fact that people were getting more and more broke)? Might it have been to prop up the automobile manufacturing industry? And would it make sense that at some time people will all (maybe only most, never all) have bought all the new cars they need, and then sales will drop? And how does this relate to the housing industry?

How about the same issue, same financial challenges, and ultimately, the same end. Home loans used to be fixed, and for thirty (30) years. Then came the adjustable, then no down with balloon payments later on, then no down, and now - no down and interest only! Again, WHY? How about because more and more people cannot qualify for normal loans? Why? They do NOT make enough money, that is why! Or, they have too much debt - or both!!! It can be argued that due to the creation of qualifying more people to make loans to, that that process has also manufactured a rise in value of homes. Perceived value, that is. Those that make large purchases today with zero down, interest only, are gambling that wages will rise, interest rates stay low, and housing continue to appreciate. According to my math (which could be in error -for I am only human), with three variables, there are six (6) possible outcomes. That being the case, the best case scenario has only a 16.6% chance of happening, meaning there is an 83.4% chance that something else will occur (that might be translated into 'losing').

Quickly, lets get a birds eye view of what happens when any of these three things do not go right:

Wages do NOT go up; interest rates are low, but housing prices continue to rise - so how does anyone with lower real income now qualify, allowing the one that bought make some money?

Interest rates DO go up: wages go up, housing prices rise, but with higher interest rates, even with interest only loans, the monthly 'nut' goes up - but can wages stay up with interest rises?

Housing does NOT appreciate: so, wages are up, interest is low - but housing is losing it value. Anyone going to buy at the old prices, or at the newer lower prices?

Many of you have read my letters concerning what I see coming in the housing industry, and also of the outsourcing challenge. Thus, my conclusion that wages will remain relatively stagnant stand; that the pronouncements of Alan Greenspan needing to raise interest rates to fight off possible inflationary actions will lead to higher interest rates, and that due to deflation, housing will indeed drop in value in the future (tied in with the decreasing viability of the R.O.I. process of the Industrial Age). Then, factor in the information shared concerning Fannie Mae and Freddie Mac and the U.S.

government's probable response to that challenge, and make your own conclusions.

The Housing Bubble will indeed burst - as the economy reacts to becoming more and more an Information Age economy. The fact that so many are dismissing the possibility of a deflationary action might be the reason to be more concerned for its actual occurrence. Remember what we have learned in this business: what we are doing is not what the majority of the citizenry of this country are doing - we are swimming against the current. I read a bumper sticker recently that might have said it all: truth is first ridiculed; then violently opposed; then accepted as having been self-evident all the time.

Read, think, analyze - and come to your own conclusions - and then act upon them. I continue to go back to what Robert Kiyosaki states so consistently: create residual income from I.P.A.!!! Each of you (the 'each' being active participants in the building of your Internet business) has the opportunity to live differently than those that do not see the future as you do. But, paraphrasing Coleman Orr, 'Opportunity without action is worth nothing'.

Remember:

KNOWLEDGE IS POWER;
IF NOT USED IT IS JUST INFORMATION.

Be a 'Seed' (meaning find a quality Mentor who will help 'raise' you), then become a Farmer to other 'Seeds'. It is in the giving of ones' self to others that one finds one self.

Farmer Ross

Chapter Six: June 2004
Week Four

HOWDY ALL!!!

Don't know where that 'Western' talk came from - must be a deep seated part of me that just escaped!!! But, sometimes we do have to let the 'inner person' out for a breath of fresh air now and then. Heard of a gal, Gussie, who was born in another part of the world. Gussie's world consisted of living in an area that was always infested with bugs and such - and so she grew up thinking that the rest of the world was the same. At any rate, after she became an adult, she had the chance to go to another country, and so she went. What she discovered was that in this new land there were no bugs whatsoever!!! And this absolutely blew her away - for all she had ever know was that bugs were a part of everyday life - and everyone just adapted to them. Now, no bugs! One might say that the world she had 'known' was true for only a number of people; but now understood that another world did exist! An outsider would view this occurrence as just an example of the truth that people only understand certain 'truths' based upon their prior experiences.

Networking; a subject that many find an uneasiness with. People join our business and are told that they must 'network' in order to build their business (and their future). Many who join would also say that they are not comfortable, nor have indulged in, the networking process. Is this true? How many of us have watched countless hours of commercials on TV (back when we used to watch TV, that is) and never thought that the person on the ad was actually 'networking' with us? Hey, did you ever see anyone else but the people in the room with you, as you watched the ads? They HAD to be talking just to you. And they were 'networking'. So, I would guess that networking is, and always has been, a natural process that we have always been involved with. Just like Gussie, maybe we discover that what we thought was a 'truth' was maybe not so much a 'truth'.

Well, maybe this sounds like some rambling - but thought I might share this idea that just came to me this day with all of you. Now, on to the news that maybe really isn't news!

1.   Ghana seeks it slice of outsourcing (Sacto Bee; 06.27.04): His room is small and hot, but he listens to cool jazz as his fingers dance across a keyboard, examining a database he's designing for one of the world's largest companies. He earns about $400 a month - $5000/year - but it is more than 10 times the average income in this small West African nation.

2.   Change in the air for malls (Sacto Bee; 06.25.04): Malls, the bastions of merchandising that for decades relied on fashion and food courts entice shopper, are losing their lids. Developers are tearing down or reconfiguring malls, making room for centers that mix traditional retailers with big-box stores, grocery stores and restaurants.

CONNECTING THE DOTS:

1. Several weeks ago (05.21.04) I sent out a note concerning the outsourcing of jobs from America. At that time India was the major player in this activity, but now it seems that other countries are involved also. Most of us would have a tough time finding Ghana on the world map - we might find it, but only because we know it is on the continent of Africa

- so we start there and look 'till we find the word 'Ghana'. But, there must be a lot of big businesses that know exactly where Ghana is, since they have people doing their work there! Did you know that the vehicle parking tickets issued to New Yorkers, are processed in Ghana!!! People in Ghana know the motor vehicle code for New York better than New Yorkers do!!! Still want to think that outsourcing is only a 'small' happening which cannot affect you or your job? Hey, when a owner of a business finds that he can get the same work done for less than 20% of what he is currently paying, do you think he will worry too much about it being done on another continent? Watch that light in your rear-view mirror: it just might be the guy or gal that will be doing your job - the job that you just 'know' cannot be done by anyone but an American!

2. Well, malls are always doing a bit of remodeling here and there, aren't they? Just a couple of years ago we who go to Arden Mall now and then witnessed a major overhaul, and we did not notice any major changes. But, now malls are being re-constructed to bring in the big-box stores, along with the specialty stores. One thing: there was no mention of Sears, or J.C. Penney, or Macy's - which are NOT big-box stores. What could be the underlying truth here? We have heard it said before that America is in the process of joining the rest of the world, as far as 'classes' of people are concerned. Might this be just another nail in the coffin of the Middle Class? Kiyosaki is quoted as saying that there are only two economic worlds to live in: the land of too little money and the land of too much money. We might say that that conforms to those that are in the 'Upper Class', and those in the 'Lower Class'. So, owners of malls know that there is now coming a time when their malls will serve only two classes of society - so the need to reconfigure them makes a lot of sense. The Middle Class IS disappearing, we just have been served with one more notice of that truth. In time, Penney's, Macys, Sears will no longer be with us - they will join the ranks of Montgomery Wards

and Weinstocks - in the bin of bankrupt businesses that tried to serve a 'class' that no longer exists.

Several years ago I came across a book in which the thesis was that the 'Red Stock' in the Stock Market was no place to be. The author shared that there are Blue Chip stocks(rich people buy their stuff), Red Chip stocks(average people buy their stuff), and White Chip stocks(mostly the lower class and poor buy their stuff) - but due to the continuing loss of people in the Middle Class, the Red Chip stocks would eventually be worth little, or nothing. The death of Montgomery Wards, which had been a Middle Class business for decades, make a case for this truth. Fearlessly, I prophesize the eventual passing of Penney's, Sears, and Macys. The Nordstrom's will co-exist in many Malls with Costco and Wal-Mart, alone with specialty stores that cater to either the Upper Class, or the Lower Class. Life will change, and people will change with it. Many who deem themselves Middle Class citizens are quickly discovering that they have more month than money; a prime qualification for membership in the Lower Class. YOU have an alternative, should you choose to take it, and use it. Pay attention to the businesses that shutter their doors, and 'connect the dots' for yourself as to why they may have done so.

Believe in yourself! There is, and always has been immense value in each of us - it is the 'world' that would keep you from discovering that fact. Find someone who is where you would want to be, and use them as your Mentor. Then, as you grow from a sprout to a thriving entity, you too - become a Mentor. The life you wish to live is found in helping others come to live the life they would wish to live.

Remember:

KNOWLEDGE IS POWER;
UNUSED IT IS JUST A BIT OF INFORMATION.

Ross

Chapter Seven: July 2004

Happy Fourth of July to all of you out there!

There was much that I found to report on this past week, but am choosing rather to focus on this truly American Holiday.

The 4th this year falls on a Sunday - which I do not remember happening for many, many years. But most of all, it falls in a time when much of what we as Americans take for granted is being challenged by many. I play in our church orchestra, and due to the fact that the 4th did fall on a Sunday our leader is presenting to the congregation, and indeed the community, a musical titled 'America, We Must Not Forget'. The music and the pictures that accompany this presentation have caused me to feel that though there is much that I could use to "connect the dots" - maybe the most important "dots" that I can share is the following.

America - there has never been another country as blessed as ours, in all of history. And the common denominator of America's personages has been the desire to be 'FREE'. Yet, today we take this commodity all too easily - having forgotten the price paid by others in earlier times.

Land of the Free, Home of the Brave; so it is stated in the song, America. Yet, how free are most Americans? It has been said that there is no freedom without economic freedom - and is there anyone among us who would disagree? Economic freedom is a 'coin' with two sides I believe; on the one side is the personal 'time' freedom that comes only with the ability of one being able to 'buy' their time back, from what used to be called a job. In being able to create a cash flow that is residual in nature, one then can be independent of any process that requires a trading of ones time for money. The other side of this 'coin' is seen in the ability to choose one's manner of creating this residual income. The 'ability' to make this choice has been paid by many, in many ways, yet it took the "Brave" who lived in this home we call America to make the supreme sacrifices. Throughout the history of America, gallant men and women can be found who made this sacrifice, most notably during World War II. Two groups that stand out in this way were the 442nd Army Battalion, made up entirely of Japanese men who made the decision to prove that America was 'their' country, by fighting. The 442nd Battalion came to be known as the Purple Heart Battalion, and was the most decorated Battalion in this war. The second group of men were the Airmen of Tuskegee. This was an all Black flight squadron, created during a darker time in Americas history when many thought that to be able to fly a plane was decided by skin color. Yet, these men took on both ignorance - and the enemy of America - and defeated both. Lives were lost in both groups, but above all, their bravery stood out in the forefront. Truly, America is the Home of the Brave. And the Brave are still giving of their lives for our Freedom. It is upon us, the recipients of this Freedom to show how we would choose to honor those that paid the ultimate price for this Freedom we sometimes so callously enjoy, and expect. Can we go out and pay the price for our own Freedom, without a loss of life, and help others gain theirs in the doing also? In the Land of the Free, we each get to make that decision. And in the making of this decision we either pay tribute to the Brave, or make their loss a payment to futility.

I hope each of us will take a few seconds, or maybe even a couple of minutes, and reflect upon the heritage of America, those that made it Free, the price they paid, and what we would do to honor their actions.

Remember:

FREEDOM IS NOT FREE!!!

Wishing to be as an Eagle, your friend and servant -

Ross

Chapter Seven: July 2004
Week Two

Summer must be here - it is July - and we are already into the last half of the year. Where DOES time go? Gotta get cooking all, for 2005 will soon be upon us - and did we not set some goals to accomplish for the year 2004? I know Linda and I did. Anyway, since I just could not get into doing the standard report last weekend - being that it was the Fourth of July - I am back, rearing to share a bunch of thoughts. So......... here we go!

1. United strikes out on loan try (Sacto Bee; 06.29.04): United Airlines lost its third and final try for a government loan guarantee when a federal board insisted that the troubled carrier could survive without one. This action will force the airline to seek new financing and throws the 1 1/2 -year old bankruptcy into doubt. Unions denounced the government decision and urged the airline to look elsewhere besides the work force for savings.

2. Off shoring issue heats up Capitol (Sacto Bee; 07.03.04): The hot-button issue of off shoring may take center stage in the Capitol next month if Gov. Arnold S. vetoes a bill that would limit the practice by state agencies. Recent actions suggest that Arnold may be leaning toward off shoring as a way to help trim the state budget. Backers of the bill say that off shoring is an inevitable part of the global economy.

3. Freddie Mac earnings plummet (Sacto Bee; 07.01.04): Mortgage giant Freddie Mac saw its earnings plummet 52%

last year amid volatile interest rates and losses as it hedged against risk while grappling with an accounting crisis. The report was delayed by the accounting problems as the government sponsored company untangled a $5 billion misstatement of earnings - mostly underreported - for 2000-2002.

4. Grocery union's leader gets a Grade A salary (Sacto Bee; 07.05.04): As president of Local 588 of the United Food and Commercial Workers in Roseville, the lifelong union man made, including "disbursements for official business", more than $567,000.

5. More pilots retire at ailing Delta (Sacto Bee; 07.07.04): Delta Air Lines' pilots union has been hit with a wave of retirements - about 300 in June - as its rank-and-file workers are expected to be asked by the struggling carrier to dig even deeper for concessions. Delta previously asked it pilots to take a 30% wage reduction and forgo a 4.5% raise they received in May. It pilots, amount the highest paid in the industry, earn between $100,000 and $300,000 a year, according to Delta.

CONNECTING THE DOTS:

1. This might be the beginning of an end. United has been a major carrier for decades - remember the TV ads with the music of Gershwin's American in Paris? Great ads - and ads that are just a part of history. United has already had it pilots take a 30% pay cut; a friend of mine who flies the 747's told me so. Wow - can you imagine taking a $75,000 a year pay cut? But, better to make $225,000 than $0, right? And the retired are also paying a price. One of 'ours' (an associate in our business) is also being affected by the challenges; the retirees may (read that WILL) be asked to pay even more of their health premiums. Retired, fixed income - and yet the cost of being retired increases. The airline industry has not much choice then to cut the frills, feed us peanuts on short

flights, sell us lunches on longer flights, and hope we, the consumer can still afford the ticket.

2. Ah, off shoring just gets more and more attention as a process to save money. And the State of California is still attempting to solve it's shortfall. An article out this day states that as things stand, next year the State will have a shortfall of some $10 Billion!!! Where will Arnold find it? People do not want to see those who are in 'need' take a hit; those with health challenges, age challenges, and such. So, then it goes to the programs such as education. But, ask any teacher when they really had their last decent raise - they do not remember! So, why not use the off shoring process in order to reduce employee cost? Hundreds of Millions, if not Billions, could be saved. At what expense? At the expense of existing jobs - and those that perform them. Another of our business associates worked for some seven years (although I think it might be closer to ten), had his position name changed, then was eliminated from State employment as a 'surplus'!!! Remember when State workers said they had 'guaranteed life-time jobs'? Not anymore. Keep your eyes open for what Arnold does with this bill - bet you he does not sign it!

3. And just why did Freddie Mac (and Fannie Mae also) underreport their earnings? As I stated in a past Money Talk, because they did not want the public to sense a 'killing' and put too much money into the system. They preferred to keep the position that income was on a positive, but general incline. They know their investors do not like wild fluctuations. What could this mean in the near future? Well, when the housing bubble does burst (and it will - have no doubt about that), then Freddie and Fannie will see challenges on their doorstep they never envisioned. And those problems will ultimately cost all of us more money. (Did you see where the median cost of a home in the Central Valley is now $400,000? A 22%

increase! There is no way this can continue - it reeks of what was happening to housing costs in 1991.)

4. Hey, what principle does this information prove? With about 24,000 members, who all pay dues, this means that the president cost each member only about $23.00 a year. Pretty cheap to get a guy that made them the best paid union people in the state. Of course, watch this next month or so as they go to the bargaining table. Remember what happened to the So Cal people? They bargained, did not like what they got, went on strike for four months, and then signed for what was basically offered four months prior. Who won? I think maybe the owners. With this as current history, do you think wages/ health care will get a whole lot better for the union people - or at best stay where it is, or at worst, get worse? Anyway, the principle that popped out at me was the one quoted by John Paul Getty: " I would rather have 1% of a hundred men's labor than 100% of my own!"

5. Probably did not need to share this one, but did so only to indicate that the challenges the old major airlines face, they all face. No doubt wages must go down - and lifestyle for many will change. Also, what of the pension plans? Many might face money challenges that they never ever believed could happen - but ultimately will.

So, what drives you today? Does the uncertainty of your job concern you? The uncertainty of your retirement? Are you aware that the number of retired individuals having to file bankruptcy continues to grow? People that grew up during the 40's and 50's, people who saved, did not get into debt, lived within their means - retired - only to find that Social Security is not that much security, that their savings cannot help much fuel their retirement when they get a whooping 1.25% return on investment, when their 401's keep turning into 201's. Find a reason to generate YOUR drive, and then put it into gear.

Take care, run hard and fast - the year is fast disappearing on all of us.

Help others find and get their dream, and you will find and get yours in the process.

Remember:

Knowledge is Power; if not used, just information.

Ross

Chapter Seven: July 2004
Week Three

Good Mooooorrrrrrrnnnnnniiiiiinnnnnnnnggggg!!!!!!

For those of you that ever saw the movie with Robin Williams in it, where he played the part of a radio reporter in Viet Nam during that conflict, - my salutation, if heard out loud, would sound like that!

At any rate, it IS a beautiful Sunday, so on to the news and dots:

1. Outsourcing is good for America - and California (Sacto Bee; 07.13.04): Suppose that tomorrow I invented a box - call it the DMV machine - which could perform every task now assigned to the Dept of Motor Vehicles, faster and at a fraction of the cost. Taxpayers would cheer because they would be paying less to provide a better product. The only ones out of sort might be the current employees of the department, who would have to find jobs in the private sector. Outsourcing also goes both ways. Just as American firms invest overseas, foreign companies also create jobs here. All this activity, even if it is ultimately positive, causes some dislocation, as people in jobs that can be done elsewhere either lose their position, or fear they might. This kind of discomfort is inevitable, a byproduct of our advancing age, ever since the buggy whip industry was extinguished by the automobile. It is not always pleasant, but that is the price paid for improving our standard of living over the past century. Assemblywoman Carol Liu of L.A. County has introduced a bill, AB1829, which would

essentially prohibit the State of Calif. from contracting with companies that provide goods and services from outside the U.S. "States and local governments should not use tax dollars to support the off shoring of service and technology when so many Americans are out of work," Liu said.

2. California school reform: Who's really for the kids? (Sacto Bee; 07.14.07): In a more reasonable world, SB 1419 would have never been proposed, let alone passed. That bill, signed into law by Gov. Grey Davis two years ago, severely restricts the ability of local school districts to contract with private providers of transportation and other non-academic school services. The cost to local school districts - could be as much as $300 million dollars a year.

3. Here's a diploma - and a big IOU (Sacto Bee; 06.28.04): Accounting students know the ramifications of taking on debt. But they also know that without debt, an eventual gain in overall earnings might be impossible. Natalie Czyz, a college accounting student in Wisconsin, estimates that she will have taken out $50,000 in students loans by the time she receives her diploma next May. Without the loans, she would not have been able to attend school and be in a position for a better paying job. Czyz could earn as much as $38,000 a year in her first year as an accountant, but will be making monthly payments on that loan of $394 for the next 25 years.

4. Frugal generation struggles with rising debt in retirement (Sacto Bee; 0711.04): America's seniors, who weathered the Great Depression or grew up in its shadow, have a reputation for frugality and saving. Yet, an increasing number of older Americans find themselves deep in credit card debt or even filing for bankruptcy. The reasons vary, but experts are saying that retirees are overwhelmed by rising medical expenses or find that Social Security and their pensions don't stretch far enough. Those who lost jobs before they were ready

to retire never quite caught up. A study has shown that the number of seniors filling for bankruptcy is still quite small - just 82,207 of them - but that group is the fastest growing group of petitioners. Howard Dvorkin says, "They are not people with lavish lifestyles, they're trying to live within their means. But, Social Security isn't cutting it for most folks."

5. Modest pay raises expected (Sacto Bee; 07.14.04): Despite an improved economy, cost-conscious employers are granting workers limited pay raises this year, and plan only slightly larger increases in 2005. Companies are budgeting about 3.3 - 3.5% - the third year in a row below the 4% level. What it comes down to is that companies are being very cost conscious.

6. Labor surplus keeps wages trailing inflation (Sacto Bee; 07.18.04): The amount of money workers receive in their paychecks is failing to keep up with inflation. There is too much slack in the labor market to generate any pressure on wage growth, said Jared Bernstein, an economist at the Economic Policy Institute. Some economists warn that if wages remain depressed for a long time they may weigh on the economy.

7.Flights of attrition (Sacto Bee; 07.17.04): "There is no doubt that the overall health of the airline industry would benefit from some carriers shutting down and going out of business," say Phillip Baggaley, Standard and Poor's airline industry analyst.

CONNECTING THE DOTS:

1. The world is in a time of massive change! Those that went from making buggy whips to helping assemble an auto faced challenges far smaller than the workers of today who go from losing a job - and then trying to find one that pays the same! Reminds me of quotes from famous people of the past, like the one who stated(concerning the number of computers

that the world would need) we would only need about five (5) of them! Maybe he meant only five - per household! Outsourcing will become a fact of our life, and that of the lives of our children. Get ready to embrace its' effect.

2. & 3. Lumping these together since they both deal with the educational system. The educational system of America changed after the Industrial Age came into being. That is when kids started 'going to school' - and the process and cost has escalated ever since. Can you imagine having a 25 year payoff so that you can just have a better job? Heck, house mortgages are only 30 years (for the time being, anyway). The costs associated with education continue to grow yearly - in California it is in the Billions of dollars - and where will it stop? My look into the future sees this: children go to elementary school; to assimilate social skills and basic learning tools (we used to call them the Three R's - reading, 'riting, 'rithmatic). From, say grade 7 on, what is now middle and high school would be taught in each kids home - over the Internet. Home schooling is becoming more and more attractive to many people - to the consternation of those that run the educational system. Think of the massive economic advantages: no buildings to maintain, no teachers to pay, no administration to pay, no transportation costs - just massive monetary savings. PLUS, each child would learn at his/her own pace! Programs are already written for much of mathematics to do this (I taught Math at Sacto High three years ago and they had these programs!). The economic challenges that our state faces will ultimately make this change occur. And the same process will eventually occur at the college level - the Internet is the medium through which change will be made.

4.,5. &6. Again, all three articles are really tied into the same challenge: no enough money! When Seniors, who were the greatest at plying the code of 'delayed gratification' are failing in retirement, what does that say to the rest of us? Wages continue to stagnant, inflation continues to grow (does the word deflation creep back into your mind?) and ominously, American Business now has more cash reserves than at any time in history!!! Microsoft has some $50Billion alone, and many other companies have their Billions also. What might they be saving all this cash for?

7. Just a continuation of a topic from last weeks Money Talk. There are six of what are called 'legacy carriers' - Delta, United Airlines, American, Northwest, Continental and US Airways. All have economic challenges in front of them - and all of them cannot continue to exist - not with the newer airlines that run so much more economically. Pilots, who make hundreds of thousands of dollars a year, have already given up some 30% of their wages, and do not want to give up more. But, even if you went from making $300,000 a year to $225,000 a year, would you walk away and quit - or still fly for say, $175,000 a year? Hmmmmmmmmmmmmm..let me think about that. Wages will continue to stagnate - and go down (see 4.,5. & 6.).

My apologies for the length of this issue - just that there was a bunch of stuff - and all related. I continue to ask the question, "Does it make sense to create residual income? And if so, is there any vehicle out there more powerful than ours?"

Take care, think, and find a direction to run in (and someone to run with you too!)

Remember:

KNOWLEDGE IS POWER;
IF NOT USED, JUST INFORMATION.

Yours in Farming!!!

Ross

Chapter Seven: July 2004
Week Four

Welcome back to 'Money Talk' - last week I found out I called it something different - 'Mooney' Talk. Not sure, but that might be a different language than English - maybe a language that is 'out of this world'!! (Moon-ey - get it?) Ok, guess I better keep my day job, since I will never make any money as a comic. But wait! I can't get a 'day job'. I found out what others are finding out today: even with several degrees from college, a wide and varied background, a work ethic unlike most - there seemed to be no need for me, since people were willing to yield what I had to offer for others that offered less - except they would work for a lot less. Hmmmmmm........ thinking I got outsourced right here in 'River City'!

Talking about thinking, what do you think of the following news:

1. Disappointing earnings send Dow below 10,000 (Sacto Bee; 07.24.04): Wall Street skidded further Friday, sending the Dow Jones back below 10,000 as disappointments deepened investors' dread of a second-half earnings slump. "You take the economic data over the last few weeks, which has been disappointing, and now all these negative earnings outlooks, and then you add in all the worries about energy prices, terrorism, Iraq, the elections - there is a lot to worry about out there," said Michael Sheldon, chief market strategist at Spencer Clarke LLC. "It is going to take a while for these issues to be resolved, and I think we'll be stuck moving sideways to lower until then."

2. Delta may seek deeper cuts from workers (USA Today; 07.22.04): Hinting that a pilots union offer of 23% pay cuts and other concessions might not be enough, Delta Air Lines said they would meet with select employees next week to lay out the carrier's worsening financial problems, warning that drastic measures are needed, since Delta reported $2Billion in losses for the second quarter. "It is painfully clear that Delta, as it is now structured, cannot survive" wrote Delta CEO Gerald Grinstein.

3. Mortgages Get More Exotic (Wall Street Journal Sunday; 07.25.04): With real-estate prices marching up relentlessly, first time buyers are finding it tough to get into the game. Who ever heard of a $500,000 starter home? Lenders have responded by devising some novel loan structures, such as: 40-year mortgage (based on the 30-year mortgage - just a slightly higher interest rate, but lower payments); Negative Amortization Mortgage (interest only allow buyers to pay LESS then the full amount of interest due); Flex-ARM Mortgage (each month the lender sends a payment coupon allowing the borrower to select four payment options, ranging from negative amortization, to 20 year fixed) - kind of like naming your own poison; Piggyback Mortgage (two mortgages - the first is for the first 80% of the loan, the second is for the remaining 20%); 103's and 107's - a no down payment loan, that allows one to borrow 3% to 7% more than the house is worth!

CONNECTING THE DOTS:

1. Wow - what a bummer of a world we live in! Challenges just coming in from every direction - and no one out there seems to have one answer to any of them. Does this seem to be something we might have heard of in the past? A year ago, ten years ago, twenty years ago - heck, how about 100 years ago? I would like to say "Do you remember when

the automobile came out and the carriage and buggy whip industry took it in the shorts"....but, as best I know none of us were around to witness that happening. But, we have heard about it; maybe in a History class from High School, maybe a History class in college, maybe we just 'heard' about it, or read about it. But, we DO know it had to have been most unsettling for those that lived through it. A disruption of lifestyle for many. And the electric light bulb, powered by generators, created to shine on streets at night time had to have left others jobless who before lit the gas lights. Wow, more un-employment!!! And all those guys and gals, who used to work on farms - well, they moved into the city to find a thing called a 'job' - whatever that was - but whatever it was it sure made life a lot more easy and fun to live. What do these happenings all have in common? They occurred right around the time the Industrial Age came into bloom - that is what! And here we find ourselves, knowing that we are now in the early "bloom days" of the Information Age - and no one expects change????? A lesson is to be learned, if we choose to learn it, from the happenings of the early 1900's (the change from the Agricultural Age to the Industrial Age); those that embrace the change will prosper - those that resist it will not. Get ready to see a part of this inevitable change as the Dow continues on a downward spiral. But, also look beyond its 'today' effect and think about what might well follow on the 'morrow'.

2.Delta, as I understand, is the most unionized air carrier in the air. And all the other legacy air carriers are making financial announcements of negative earnings also. What if you found yourself, having worked for some business for 21 years, and then find the business failing - and maybe going out of business? How would you feel? Mad? Hurt? Peeved? (Industrial Age word) Lost? Feeling a sense of hopelessness? Whatever you would feel, most assuredly you would not feel very upbeat. I am sure that our hearts go out to all those that work in this industry - yet there is little any of that we can do to abort the changes that must, and will, occur. Could we each use this happening as a personal lesson - a lesson that will only reinforce our knowledge of why we spend time in another business, apart from our 'day job' business, to help insure that we and our families will not have to feel this type of pain?

3. OK Gals and Guys (know that usually we see it as 'guys and gals' - but do not wish to sound chauvinistic) - TEST TIME!!! I know how I would 'connect the dots' on this one - but I am only one mind - and I want and need to hear other minds. So, become a part of this program - and tell me how YOU 'connect the dots' on this one. I will not use last names, but will use first names in sharing your thoughts.

That old song, The Time's They Are A' Changing, is so true in the world we live in today. Embrace change, use it to your advantage, and live well and prosper (Spock would have said the same thing!).

Remember:

KNOWLEDGE IS POWER;
IF NOT USED, JUST INFORMATION.

Finding Significance through the Success of Others,

Ross

Chapter Eight: August 2004

Hey, this Seminar WAS outstanding - and Estella Salinas - if you have ever listened to her before, she was as good as ever - and if you have not had the chance to do so, get her tape/CD or even better - her video. Words fail when it comes to this what and how this Lady shares thoughts.

And, after the 'Event' (hey, it might cost me $5 to say the 'f' word! - for those of you that did not make it, talk to someone who did and they can fill you in on the 'f-word' thingy) Linda and I took a small vacation, heading to Universal Studio for a day, and then for some extra rest, then home. And, ready to hit the highways and biways like never before!!!

Thus, I could not send out the usual Sunday edition, and this short, but hopefully impactful one, will do.

On to the news:

1. Small financial shock, very large earthquake (Financial Times, 08.02.04); John Plender (www.ft.com/plender), the author of this article states...."....it will take a smaller shock to derail markets now than at any time in recent memory because everyone is in hock to an unprecedented degree. The story of the decade thus far has, after all, been one of US monetary policy trying to offset the contradictionary impact of the equity market slide by blowing bubbles in housing and corporate and securitized debt that have reverberated around the world. With US short rates at 1.25% and rising, the fun is over. But

leverage is not, with large investment banks taking on more risk, due to declining profits and low market volatility. We have a system overloaded with debt in the household and public sectors and stretched by financial imbalances. Whether it happens in August is anyone's guess, but something nasty is certainly around the corner." [Insert the phrase 'house price crash' into the Google search bar, and you will learn of no less than 1.07m references to the impending deluge.]

CONNECTING THE DOTS:

1. Many that I talk with do not see any impending change - they feel that yes, there will be a 'correction' as has occurred in 1991, and prior 'housing crash years', but that it will rebound. Sadly, my position is that the rebound they 'count on' will never be witnessed. Too much debt, too stagnant of wages, lowering of R.O.I., outsourcing, job losses, etc. Discretionary income will become less and less to the average household while non-discretionary spending will increase with inflation. Maybe I am wrong, but sure seems to look like a classic deflationary picture. Additionally, the International Monetary Fund (IMF) is now telling the US that its debt is too high and must be addressed; by lowering spending and raising taxes!!! This is the first time I know of where a world body told the United States what to do. Ominous???

As for the 'house price crash' plug, I went into Google last night to insure that the author of this article was accurate on his number of references. Now, he wrote this article on August 2, and last night (August 3) when I did the search I did not find 1,070,000 references; I found 1,080,000!!! Ten thousand increase in only one day. And today, when sharing this info with a friend, I did not find the 1,080,000 references, but 1,090,000!!! An additional 10,000 references in one day! Now, I do not know about you, but something sure seems afoot. And this crash will affect not only the US, but the UK and Australia as well - and no doubt a host of other nations as well. Change IS afoot. Be ready for it.

Gals and Guys - I am by nature one of the most optimistic people in the world, but that does not mean I see everything through a blue lens. Change is coming - have no doubt about that - for change is always in the wind. The one key that I see to getting through these coming changes is by having more money coming in than you need to live on. Residual income IS the only means of doing so. So, get out there, quit messing around, and build the business that is at your feet. For, what if I am truly in error - none of my forecasts come to life, what then? Well, given that you did build your business to a point of financial freedom - who cares if I was wrong! I surely won't - for Linda and I will have found our financial freedom by helping others gain theirs too. We can't lose this ball game - so we would be less than ......something........to not have done it. It is a WIN-WIN situation for each of us.

PLAY BALL!!!

Remember:

KNOWLEDGE IS POWER;
IF NOT USED IT IS JUST INFORMATION.

Ross

Chapter Eight: August 2004
Week Two

Well, did all of you recover yet from the Seminar???

Some of us needed more than one or two days to get over the 'after effects' - and lets face it, any ol' reason is a good reason for a vacation! Yet, it was the invigoration that we ended up with that we really had to recuperate from - can't run any engine at extremely high RPM for ever - got to let it cool down now and then. But, now that we are done 'cooling down' , time to rev up again. So, gonna start to build up the RPM's a bit at a time, and so I start the engine once more:

1. Shoppers' spending again tight (Sacto Bee; 08.06.04): New York - Consumers' frugal spending extended into a second month during July, giving many retailers lackluster sales gains, particularly at apparel chains including Gap Inc. and midpriced department stores. As retailers announced their monthly results Thursday, the bright spots were luxury merchants and discounters such as Wal-Mart.

CONNECTING THE DOTS:

1. How should this headline have been truly written? This is the challenge I speak about - so many 'titles' of articles mention the 'beginning of a trip, and the end of a trip, but NEVER what the trip was truly about. In my mind, the headline should have been: 'Another piece of evidence that the Middle Class is disappearing.'

What is read, is that the 'luxury' merchants (might that be the Nordstrom's of the world?) and discounters (Wal-Mart for sure, but including Sam's Club, Costco, etc) had a good, or very good, month, while the J.C. Penney's, Sears, Gaps, etc., had what could be called a 'miserable' month. But, who shops where? Do you know of any who make minimum wage shopping at Nordstrom's? Or, how about those making just a couple of thousand dollars a month spending their hard earned (and minimal) dollars there either? Then again, do you know of individuals who make $4-5000 plus, a month, going to Wal-Mart? No, the ones you see there (mostly) are the ones that cannot afford Nordstrom's due to lack of income excess.

How can we start to feel (know?) that the Middle Class is starting to disappear? Let us look at the parameter of 'wage increase' over the past several years. It is now well known and written about weekly ,in daily newspapers, that wages/salaries have only gone up some 3-4% a year; and for a lot of years now! What you who are reading this most probably realize is that inflation has been around 6%+ for the last 40 years - and has not really changed! What did change is the manner in which our government economists calculate inflation. Since homes, transportation, medical, food and clothing are not usually factored into the calculation of inflation, is it any wonder that we are told that inflation is only about 2% or so? Let's get real! Housing has gone up over 20% here in the Sacrament area for the past two years - yet is totally ignored in the calculation of true inflation. Don't know about you, but when Linda and I go house shopping, the numbers are staggering.

Then, let us look at discretionary and non- discretionary spending. In the end, would you agree that no matter what you buy, no matter in what category the 'stuff' you buy fits in, either you have the money or you do not. And if you do not, then I guess you charge it - only making a bad situation worse, ultimately. And, if your income has become stagnant (meaning to me that your wage increase IS about the real inflationary rate (6%+/-), or is less than stagnant (wages only went up 2-4%), what you spend is what you have. And, given your 'real' spending has less value, then you spend where it goes farther. People who make BIG BUCKS usually keep making BIG BUCKS, and spend where BIG BUCKS let you spend (Nordstrom's and such). Those who sense their money is not going as far as it once did, find another place to shop, rather than J.C. Penney's and Sears or The Gap - they go to big-box discounters. And what is the result?

Middle Class stores get less business - and then go out of business. Witness Montgomery Wards, Macys, etc. Watch the coming demise of Sears and J.C. Penney's, and other Middle Class venues. What, ultimately, does this prove?

That Robert Kiyosaki was, and is, 100% correct. People will ultimately end up living in only one of two 'lands': The Land of Too Little Money, or the Land of Too Much Money. You are going to witness the proof of his words. The question each of us must ask is this: Which Land do I wish to live in?????? And given you make your answer, 'what are you willing to do to get there'? (Of course, if you chose the Land of Too Little Money, you are probably already there and have to do nothing.) And if you choose not to answer either way today, then realize that in reality you DID answer! You choose to live in the Land of Too LITTLE Money. In not choosing, you choose, whether you realize it or not! And would you agree that it will take more work to live in the land of Too Little Money, than the work it would have taken to live in the Land of Too Much Money, since by choosing to live in the Land of Too Little Money - that choice demands that you work many, many years, decades - and maybe till you 'run out of gas'. On the other hand, since those that live in the Land of Too Much Money do so only due to their residual income, by definition of residual income, they only did their work one time.

Life is choice; choose well - but choose quickly and implement your action of choice immediately.

As for me and mine, we choose the Land of Too Much Money ('cause at heart I am really pretty lazy!)

Remember:

KNOWLEDGE IS POWER;
IF NOT USED, ONLY INFORMATION.

Farmer Ross

Chapter Eight: August 2004
Week Three

Some days life is a challenge; some days life is a party; and some nights are just too good - like last night up at Charlie and Christy's home where many of those that met the latest business Incentive!!! Charlie B-B-Q'd the tri-tip and chicken to perfection, lots of goodies and drink (all non-calorie bearing, mind you) from the land of XS - and most of all - the best association one could find. People all over the place talking with one another they don't get a chance to see all that often, kids - yeah, kids playing like crazy having fun; just one good time. Funny, we did what we were going to do, business-wise, to make it there - and then we just plain enjoyed ourselves. Being around all these great folk sure shows the difference we get to enjoy in being around people whose values and goals we all share in common. If you did not make it last night, then you do need to plan to make it to the next one. Now, on to the story of the week:

1. What to do as Consumers Cut Back (Wall Street Journal Sunday, 08.15.04): The U.S. consumer is showing signs of weakening, finally. And that could leave the stock market, and the economy, in a fragile position. The past few years the U.S. economy has been powered by the strength of consumer spending, as a tumble in interest rates allowed them to shave monthly mortgage payments and re-duce credit card debt. Yet, this key part of the economy could be under some pressure, raising questions about the stock market. The Dow Jones Industrial Average is essentially flat, now down 6% for

the year. And, there are solid reasons for concern: retail sales were mixed, the Fed has raised interest rates and indicated that more raises are coming, and now job jitters about employment, all indicators that the economy has slacked off it blistering growth rate during the first half of the year. For investors, the quandary is whether the economy is just going through a 'soft patch', or whether years of piling up debt and saving too little is forcing consumers to slow spending.

CONNECTING THE DOTS:

1. Well, we see it in print, indicating that someone else out there sensing a challenge with the economy. Admission that consumer spending, tied to raising interest rates and job losses, might be lending itself to a slowdown of the economy. Last week I noted yet one more 'report' that speaks to the loosing of a long-standing tier of the three-class system we all have grown up in: the middle class. In a magazine supplement in the Sacto Bee today (Parade) there was a piece on those out there without any health insurance at all - and that the government should have, or should be, doing something about it. And do you think you might know what group of people most populate this segment of our population? Yup, of course they were not mentioned by 'class' - but with inference by the amount of money they make - the Middle Class. The U.C. (Upper Class) have all the money they need to purchase their own health insurance, the L.C. (Lower Class) have a bunch of Medi-aids, and those finding themselves in the M.C. (you can figure this one out), with jobs, yet no health insurance provided, and not making enough to pay for it and other non-discretionary items. I have shared my personal speculation on the stock market with many, and I re-state it now: I see the market ultimately going down to around 6,000 to 8,000, closer to 6 than to 8, in the future. For at that point the R.O.I. will then come to a more favorable number of 6-8%+/yearly,

then the anemic 2-3% now. Yet, one-half of the value of the market will disappear to make this happen. Same thing will no doubt occur with housing: homes selling for $500,000 in time will sell for $300,000; and all that 'money' will disappear too, yet still be owed.

A thought popped into my head as I was starting to write this weeks edition: is it possible that as our economy changes as we go deeper into the Information Age, that even the concept of making money (of how one does that) will change also? Wal-Mart continues it assault on the price of 'stuff' - and one would accept the fact that there has to be a 'floor' which cannot be broken through - the 'floor' of the cost to just make it and make a bit of profit. Yet, this 'floor' might also be 'broken thru' via the lowering of the wages of the employees. We see this occurring today with Delta Air Lines and American Air Lines, where the pilots are offering yet more wage concessions in order to keep their jobs! Maybe this does not make any sense to some of you out there (maybe it doesn't make any sense to any of you!) - but change is coming. And all I have learned is that we do not want to make the mistake of assuming that what used to work will continue to work in the same manner. For is that not one reason that many of us have started our own business, using a variant business model that never came to full acceptance during the Industrial Age (though it worked might well for those that embraced it - but WILL be the business model of the Information Age - all due to the nature of the Internet. Oh well, if this side-bar has given any of you something to think about - and reply to me about - that would be nice. Hearing from you and your thoughts, for it is only through the interchange of ideas that any of us can move ahead.

Well, stick a fork in it - for it is done!

Remember:

KNOWLEDGE IS POWER;

AND IF NOT USED, JUST INFORMATION.

Find a Mentor, Follow your Mentor, and Become a Mentor to others!

Farmer Ross

Chapter Eight: August 2004
Week Four

Just back from making our annual pilgrimage to the California State Fair - and of course, that means spending a few bucks on some outrageous food - and of course, that means also spending some outrageous money for the outrageous food! And, Lin and I go to see what might be new, some of what is always old - but familiar - and maybe just one new thing! And the one new thing I found was the food; thank goodness for that - can you imagine eating food that was a year old? Ok, just one more piece of proof that if I want to live in the Land of Too Much Money, I had better concentrate on my Internet business - and not seek remuneration as a 'comic'!!!

And speaking of living in the Land of Too Much, or Too Little, Money - let me segue into the news that we witnessed this past week:

1. Income Gap is Growing in U.S. (Sacramento Bee; 08.17.04): Over two decades, the income gap steadily has increased between the richest Americans, and those at the middle and bottom of the pay scale, whose paychecks buy less. The growing disparity is even more pronounced in this recovering economy. Wages are stagnant, and the middle class is shouldering a larger tax burden. Prices for health care, housing, tuition, gas and food have soared.

2. What Happens if Promised Pensions can't be Delivered? (Sacramento Bee; 08.17.04): During the 1988 presidential election campaign, the savings and loan industry was

a rotting onion. Dukakis, the Democratic candidate, mentioned it once, but was told to cool it because the smell would stick to both parties. After the election, the onion was peeled, resulting in almost $200 billion being paid out then, and we still are paying for it as a small part of the $179 billion paid out this year in interest on loans to cover federal debt. During this election, pension insurance is the rotting onion, and the social effects could be much worse than the economic effects of the S&L scandal. Companies that offered a defined benefit retirement program, it insures it with the federal Pension Benefit Guarantee Corp. The PBGC pays only a portion of what the retirees were due. Today, the PBGC is seriously sick itself - being technically broke. Cash strapped United Airlines just skipped a $72 million quarterly payment to its pension plan. At the end of last year, the PBGC was $11.2 billion in the hole.

CONNECTING THE DOTS:

1. Think I wrote about this situation in the last month or so - but in reality, it is not anything that should amaze anyone any longer. The Rich have always gotten richer, and thus - the Poor had to get more poor. And why is this, one might ask? Well, read Rich Dad, Poor Dad and CashFlow Quadrant, and you will find out. For those that need to read these books, but have not yet done so, I will share the answer as Robert Kiyosaki lays it out: the Rich get the rules written, called 'laws', and everyone not 'rich' abides by them. And of course, as Dale Carnegie shared some 60 years ago in his book, How to Win Friends and Influence People, the most important person in anyone's life is: (drum roll.....................) him or her self! So now you know why (if you did not already know) the Rich get richer. And, notice that we are hearing more and more that wages ARE stagnant. And, did you notice the list of 'stuff' that has gone up? Each of them is NOT factored into

the cost of living - which the government calls 'inflation'. So if most think inflation is a mere 2% +/-, and wages go up an average of 3%+/-, those that do not 'think' - think they are getting ahead financially - yet their check book tells them another story! One more piece of proof that those that choose to live by the wage (trading time for money) will continually find their financial situation going downhill! The monetary reward for having the typical A-system job will lead most all, ultimately, to living in the Land of Too LIttle Money.

2. I find it great that someone is finally taking notice of this challenge facing Americans. Those that are all ready retired and living on some sort of defined benefit pension need to take notice: things WILL ultimately change for them. American Airlines has just gone on record as saying they will NOT be paying any more money into their pension plan, for they need to jettison (no pun there!) this cost to get out of bankruptcy. My feeling is that you WILL witness the bankruptcy of both American Airlines and Delta, at a minimum - for there are other 'legacy' airlines facing the same financial situations. And those that receive, or will receive, their pension dollars from American, will ultimately get fewer of them from the PBGC, and probably combined with a higher health payment due from these pensioners also. The social effects of this 'rotting onion' WILL traverse America - from coast to coast - and only those living in the Land of Too Much Money will live well at all.

Some of you may feel that I am being a bit 'pushy' on this idea of life existing for all in only one of two 'Lands', in the near future. And, I will hereby join you in saying this is TRUE!!! I will continue to PUSH; push your thinking from thinking as you have been taught to think in Industrial Age thinking processes to thinking as Robert Kiyosaki teaches - in Information Age thinking. If you ask me exactly what Information Age thinking is, I can not tell you - we are witnessing its birth, just as those that lived during the change of Ages from the Agricultural Age into the Industrial Age. What few of them realized is that 'things were changing' - and that those that accepted the change, and embraced the change, came out on top. We, who live in this time, are living in the time of transformation from the Industrial to the Information Age. Those of us who accept the truth that residual income will be the ONLY way for the average person to live well, and create residual income, WILL live in the Land of Too Much Money. Any that disagree with this thought - show me how I might be wrong - and if you do your 'due diligence, you might just find the proof YOU need to get YOU moving faster than YOU are in building your business. This is NOT about me being right - it is more important that YOU know that what YOU are doing is what YOU should be doing - even if that means going after another degree from college, or going after a better paying job. In the end, YOUR decisions HAVE to be YOURS. I only implore YOU to make sure that the decision YOU make is founded upon as much truth as YOU can find to support YOUR decision.

Remember:

KNOWLEDGE IS POWER;

IF NOT USED IT IS MERELY INFORMATION.

Find a MENTOR; Follow your MENTOR; Become a MENTOR.

Farmer Ross

Chapter Eight: August 2004
Week Five

The manner in which we live, the aspects of how we live, and maybe even how long we live, continues to be defined. Science continues to usher in processes that enhance the span of one's life - and the economy is ushering in more and more challenges in how we will live during these additional years we pick up. During the past several months you have read the headlines of how pension plans are beginning to falter, the on-going joke of 401's turning into 201's (and less), the downward spiral of returns within the stock market, the minimal creation of well paying jobs, the stagnation of wages. What does it all mean? In truth, no one can truly say; what they can do is to speculate - with that speculation based upon history. Get ready for some 'zippy days' is what I would admonish.

So, what headlines do I have today - that embellish upon the challenges that continue to crop up? Here are a couple for your reading - and cogitation:

1. Some experts see signs of a long bearish streak (Sacto Bee; 08.28.04): If you're a stock investor, lately you might feel you are swimming against a current and not getting very far. The market's sideways moves since that start of the year have frustrated Wall Street professionals too, leading some experts to think the current pattern is part of a much larger, bearish trend.

2. Census: Poverty rose by million (USA Today; 08.27.04): The number of Americans in poverty and without

health insurance each rose by more than 1 million in 2003, the Census Bureau reported. Also, the income of the median U.S. household was virtually flat at $43,318, after a two year decline. The results were expected, coming after timely reports showing higher long-term unemployment, slow wage growth and surging health care costs in 2003.

CONNECTING THE DOTS:

1. Sad to say, I tire of continuing to report on the lack of a decent return within the Stock Market sector of our economy. Yet, this will continue to be a major headline, week in and week out in the coming months. Watch how the economy is brought into the Presidential election - each party will say two things: 1) that the other party has helped create this situation, and: 2) that they have the answer. Each party is correct on statement 1: yes, both parties did help create the situation. And, each party is mostly wrong on statement 2: for in truth, no one truly knows what the answer is to this situation - since they really do not know what the cause is. Just know one thing: the market will continue to pay out lousy returns on the investment made by stock holders.

2. So the government has some more proof that the poor are growing in numbers - yet they will not say where this bunch of people are coming from! Seems like either they come from the rich neighborhoods, or the middle class neighborhoods - and my guess is the latter!!! Would you agree that if you have wage stagnation, and inflationary movement on non-discretionary spending, that many in the middle class would be forced down into the lower class? And also, realize that the 'median' number is that number of which there are an equal number above as below. So, there are an equal number of people making more than this $43,318 as there are below. And $43,318 yearly income means an average monthly income of $3609.83. Figure that a family only takes home about 75%

(maximum) of their gross pay that means that there is only $2707.38 spendable income. How in the world does one buy a home for $300,000.00 with this income? Oh well, guess it doesn't matter if one can really AFFORD to make these payments, only if they can QUALIFY to do so.

And the above is my segue into my concluding thoughts for this week:

Came across a paper by an economist by the name of James Shepherd, who has a business advising clients on stock market positions. In this paper, Shepherd writes about an Economic Winter, and another late (meaning really dead) economist who lived until 1939, named Kondratieff, who did much research and speculation on this idea of an Economic Winter. Basically, the thesis is that the free enterprise system has its ups and downs, but ultimately because of major ups (excesses in money making), there would follow a major down (economic winter) that would purge these excesses and then the cycle would start again. In fact, Kondratieff studied this action from the 1760-s through the 1930's. According to this theory, we were due a major down in 1987 - yet it did not occur. But, many of the conditions required for this 'down' are now present. You see, the 1929 stock market crash was NOT the cause of the great depression: the descent into a deflationary spiral was. This condition I have written about months ago in prior Money Talks. That deflationary environment pulled the economy into the abyss that devastated the value of most assets, including stocks and real estate. I believe that we will have another crash - call it an economic winter or whatever - but it will happen! Contributing to this feeling is the immense rise in price of residential real estate, brought about by the lowest interest rates we have witnessed in the past several decades. This leads to record levels of debt, and will contribute to a meltdown of the economy. Either the building crash will precipitate the market crash, or the market crash will precipitate the building crash. One WILL occur, and then the other will follow. Those that are able to see that this can occur, and prepare for it, will come out the winner. Those that do not - well, bad news. Again, the historian that said 'those that do not learn from history are doomed to repeat it' will be proved most correct.

A last thought: we all live in the greatest nation that history has ever recorded - but that does not infer that we have always been correct in all that we (as a nation) do or say. One might ask, "If the government (read that Greenspan) knows that massive economic changes are afoot, why would they not tell us?" Think about it. The power that Greenspan has, within his utterances, could cause chaos in the market place. What good would that do our nation? None, as I see it. Better for the masses to muddle through it, day by day, with minimal chaos for the government to worry about. In the end, we - yes WE, are the final arbiters of our destiny. Each of us, you and I, have the power to make our choices. You know that the choices you made five years ago have dictated how you live today. You have that power. You either make a choice, and act on it, or have a choice made for you (by your not making a choice you make a choice!). If the common denominator of our existence is based upon this medium we call money, then would it make sense to get our butts in gear and do what we need to do to insure that WE stay as much in control of our lives as possible? By aligning ourselves with the business model we are in, we might well be doing the only way thing any of us can do to become masters of our own destiny. If you can find another way, more powerful and quicker and honest and ethical than this combined duo, then let all of us know! But, to do so you would have to prove Frank Feather incompetent - for Frank made the declaration over a year ago that what his studies indicate our business model would be "the Sun around which all the other Internet businesses would revolve." You want to be the 'bulls-eye' or what?

Remember:

KNOWLEDGE IS POWER;
IF NOT USED IT IS JUST INFORMATION.

Find a Mentor; Use your Mentor; Become a Mentor!

Farmer Ross

Chapter Nine: September 2004

Happy Holidays to each of you!

This weekend finds us enjoying (I hope you are enjoying it!) what has been called the 'Last Holiday of Summer' - Labor Day. And what a fitting name - Labor day - for history will show that more 'labor' longer, and for less return (monetarily speaking), today than ever before. I also recognize that this holiday was created to honor 'labor' (if my memory serves me well) - but also when honest 'labor' led to a respectful conclusion. By this I mean a quality time of retirement. Today, as will be shortly exhibited by news stories from this past week, many will never know 'quality retirement time'. So, now that I have you 'bummed out' about where a majority of working people are headed, let's really get you 'bummed out' with the facts:

1. Public may face a big pension bill (Sacto Bee; 08.30.04): It's white-knuckle time for airline shareholders, workers and creditors as major carriers fight to pull out of their financial tailspin. Taxpayers should be worried too. They (the taxpayers) could be in for a very bumpy ride if carriers seek bankruptcy protection and transfer their $31 billion worth of pension liabilities to the Pension Benefit Guaranty Corp. The PBGC, the federally backed insurance agency that protects the private retirement plans of more than 44 million workers, is running a deficit of $9.7 billion after years of absorbing the pension obligations of bankrupt employers. Piling on the aviation industry's obligation could overwhelm the system and

potentially lead to a massive, taxpayer-funded bailout. United Airlines has said it plans to skip nearly $500 million in pension contributions this fall. US Airways may be on the brink of insolvency again.

2.   Pensions put San Diego in fiscal hole (Sacto Bee;09.02.04): San Diego - this city is caught in a financial crisis of colossal proportions. A problem not caused by a downturn in the economy, nor a bad deal with a pro football team, nor one caused by a cutback in state support - although a problem caused by pieces of all of the above. San Diego's financial problem is largely one of it's own making. By under funding its public employee pension program, the city is now so deeply in the red, that pension payments will virtually suck the treasury dry. The shortfall is $1.157 billion - and growing.

3. The Next Shock: Not Oil, but Debt (The New York Times; 09.05.04): With oil prices hovering above $40 a barrel, experts have calmed frayed nerves by noting that today's services-driven American economy is much less addicted to the black stuff than yesterday's industrial economy (hey - another writer that understands we are NO LONGER in the Industrial Age! - my comment here). That's the good news. The bad news is that other recent structural changes in the economy - the federal government's shift from surpluses to huge deficits, the national predilection for consumption over savings - and housing prices that climb faster than income - have increased the country's reliance on another kind of fuel: credit. The economy's apparent reliance on credit to fuel everything from home buying to the military budget is troublesome. If incomes and revenues fail to rise, stressed consumers may have a tough time keeping up with payments. An economy hooked on debt is also vulnerable to the inevitable rise in interest rates. Rising interest rates will mean more of one's income will be

spent on debt service, leaving less for consumption. The bigger the debt, the smaller the margin for error.

And now, just to finish you off:

4. Always on the Job, Employees Pay With Health (New York Times; 09.05.04): American workers are stressed out, and in an unforgiving economy, they are becoming more so every day. Sixty-two percent say their workload has increased over the last six month; fifty-three percent say work leaves them "overtired and overwhelmed." It is enough to make workers sick - and it does. Decades of research have linked stress to everything from heart attacks an stroke to diabetes and a weakened immune system. It is an issue everywhere you go in the world, says Dr. Guy Standing in a report from the International Labor Office, an agency of the U.N. The traditional career, progressing step by step through the corridors of one or two institutions, "is finished," said Dr. Richard Sennett, a sociologist at New York University. He has calculated that a young American today with at least two years of college can expect to change jobs at least 11 times before retirement. Business has moved away from traditional employment, now an almost quaint concept - and today one finds that one in every four workers in the U.S. is "in some nontraditional employment relationship," including part-time work and self-employment.

CONNECTING THE DOTS:

Ok, you can get off the floor now - you still have tomorrow to rest (or at least I hope you have Monday off!). I truly believe that the four articles I have just cited constitute the hardest hitting of any one-weeks-stuff I have written about, as a whole. But, let's see what the 'dots' might have to say.

1. More and more you will both read and hear about this situation. It is NOT going away - it will just become a larger and larger challenge. As I see it, many - maybe all - of what are called the 'legacy carriers' will ultimately be doomed to just a part of history - for they will pass away. As written just a week or so ago, other 'legacy' carriers are also having their financial challenges - and one method of temporarily meeting them will be to forgo their pension plan payments. Ultimately, the PBGC will have more names added to their list of payees - but where will the money come from? That seems to be a no-brainer. Can the U.S. government allow the presence of tens of millions of retired workers living on S.S.S. alone - meaning that they would be living in a level of poverty? So, one more bail-out .... and paid for by......you insert the group name (hint: it rhymes with 'jacks-payer). And where does this additional money come from, courtesy of the 'jacks-payer'? Oh, out of their not needed discretionary income. Sorry for sounding facetious, but it oooozed out. Just know that YOU will NEED more money to live just the way you live today - and if that is not well enough - then you just have to find a way to earn MORE money.

2. For all those that hear, or say and believe, the mantra that 'government pensions are guaranteed' - let's see how this situation plays out in San Diego. For this is a PUBLIC pension that we are witnessing having challenges. And if they are having challenges, might it make sense to think that other PUBLIC pension plans are experiencing the same challenges? Several months ago I wrote about the situation here in Sacrament County - bet their auditors are staying up late at night to see where they are heading. But, the saddest truth is that it is honest, hard-working former employee's (and current ones also) that might end up taking the brunt of the challenge -

meaning learning to live on less - or going back and getting another job.

3. DEBT! I think debt is like an illness - with many out there hoping there is a simple and easy cure to rid one's self of it. Sad to say, the cure is simple - but not very easy. In fact, there are two cures for this illness: the first is to just not spend what you do not have to spend; and the second is to make more than you do spend. Don't know if one is easier than the other - but if there is no difference, then I would choose to just make more than I need, for then lifestyle will just get better and better! But whooooa, the article was about this new 'fuel' Americans have found. Trouble is, this 'fuel' is just like oil - only worse, since oil has a finite volume, and God is not making any more that I know of. But money, now this is a different horse! As Mac (McCracken, for those that are new to this business) has so profoundly taught us, there is "no short-age of money, and never will be". Not with the credit cards in your back pocket - or for you Ladies out there - the cards in your purse (and you can hold a whole lot more of them than a guy with a tiny wallet - and no, this is not a barb - about women, just a fact - purses are usually larger than a wallet! - about right now Linda is saying "Ross - get back on track and off these rabbit trails!"). Getting off course, sorry about that. Again, America is financed up to it's neck in debt, through re-fi's, credit cards, you name it. And this 'illness' will soon be soon to be worse than most believe.

4. But, you already knew this - for don't you come home tired, wishing for a longer vacation - maybe even wishing for no job - just a slower pace of life? And what do the studies show? That the vaunted degree's which so many of us in the past chased, and caught, are no longer a 'glue' that would ce-ment us to positions higher in the chain we work in, nor even can glue us to where we are already. Eleven jobs during a work career - and we are no doubt talking about a work career that

will span more than 40 years - maybe like 50 for the 'just getting started' in their careers. And to what end? If you are not sure, re-read items 1 and 2 above. Please, do not use parents or older successful people out there as your measuring stick - for they grew up and worked in an entirely different 'culture' than exists today. What worked for them WILL NOT work for you. And by that I mean the process of a 'job' - not of having a good work ethic and such. That old acronym of job: Just Over Broke will sadly be proved many times over in the coming days. I have a good friend who just yesterday was talking to me, wondering why - after getting his college degree, being a quality worker for the State (California), and then being phased out - he could not get a decent job after TWO YEARS. I shared with him it was not of his making, for at 45 he had too much qualification for an employer to hire him, feeling that since he was so qualified he would leave quickly after finding a better paying job. Or, that an employer could find a younger, and thus cheaper, employee. The rules changed. Reminds me of that book, Who is Watching Your Cheese (or Eating it, or something). Someone can get back to me with the correct name - but I would recommend all of you reading it if you have not yet done so.

The changes that each of us will witness will come ten times faster than occurred during the Industrial Age. Do not be surprised that all this 'stuff' seems to be happening so quickly. As the Boy Scouts so aptly say: Be Prepared! Do not be like the grasshopper, putting off the hard work 'till later - hoping there will be time to prepare for the Winter. Be as the Ant - and get the work done and over with. Then, when Winter comes (which it will), you can just sit by your fireplace, with a nice fire roaring (well, maybe must meowing), you with a cup of Hot Chocolate in your hands, rocking your rocker, enjoying the sounds of the raindrops as they hit your roof. Cozy. Warm. Content.

Take advantage of what you do know, what you have at your fingertips, and the Mentors that are willing to give you their 'all'. It is said that most people only have a Great Opportunity given to them once in a life-time. The decision is to find out if you are either an Ant - or a Grasshopper. Time will tell.

Enjoy the coming days, for they will find you busier than ever.

Remember:

KNOWLEDGE IS POWER;
IF NOT USED, JUST INFORMATION.

Find a Mentor, Use a Mentor, Become a Mentor.

Farmer Ross

Chapter Nine: September 2004
Week Two

Hello to all of you on a Sunday that feels just a tad bit like Fall!!! The weather is beautiful - not too hot, and definitely not cold. Linda and I went to breakfast downtown, ate outside in a most enjoyable setting (Tower Cafe), and even met the couple sitting next to us - and Voila! - could you see it coming? This couple is seeking residual income!!! Will be getting together soon no doubt with the ultimate in residual income. And what did we talk about? Well, how about the first item in this weeks Money Talk:

1. Faith in company pensions falls (Sacto Bee;09.12.04): Retirees and workers who have toiled for their companies for decades have long viewed their pensions as money in the bank. Now, some are beginning to wonder just how secure they really are.

2. Employer insurance cost go up 11.2% (USA Today;09.10.04): The cost of health insurance provided by employers rose an average of 11.2% this year and is expected to rise again in 2005, adding to the economic anxiety of workers and businesses. It is the fourth straight year of double-digit increases. As the cost employers pay goes up, so do dollars workers pay toward their coverage. This year workers paid an average of $2691 toward a family policy, and many are also paying more for deductibles and co-payments. Fifty-two percent of the large employers surveyed said they were very likely to increase the amount workers pay for insurance.

3. Airlines awash in red ink (Sacto Bee; 09.11.04): Three years after terrorists used jetliners as weapons and sent commercial aviation into its worst slump ever, the airline industry remains mired in red ink and is facing dramatic change. With few exceptions, the major carriers are in critical financial shape - still losing money, even though the summer is the airlines' busiest season. In all, the carriers have lost a collective $27 billion since the attacks.

CONNECTING THE DOTS:

1. Last week I wrote about the San Diego public pension challenge; months ago I wrote about the challenge Sacramento County is likely to face, and now it comes to light that people are fearing that their company pensions may also fail them. The good news is that people are starting to notice that the 'sky might be falling' after all. The tired old mantra of 'guaranteed pension' might be wearing thin around the edges for many. For ultimately, what does 'guaranteed' really mean? For a numerical value (the number of dollars a system says it will pay each month) is a far different critter than the number of dollars required to live decently. By this I mean that money has a 'time value'. You have all heard of inflation, and no doubt know that if a dollar suffers a 6% inflationary rate over one year, then what $1 dollar bought this year will take $1.06 to buy the next. So, if someone knows that if they work for another 12 years, and are told they will receive $4000 a month at retirement, and inflation is 6% for the next 12 years, that $4000 (that seems to be a goodly number today) will only buy $2000 worth of stuff in 12 years (and $2000 is not what one might call a 'goodly' number today!). Thus, it is a good thing that people are starting to do some thinking about their pension plans - whether they exist in the coming years, and also what they truly will be worth.

2. Of course, most of us do not have to worry about this occurrence. Especially since health costs are not factored into the inflationary rate. Heck, another part-time job will just about cover the increases; and wouldn't it be just peachy to be able to welcome all those savers into your local Wal-Mart? OR: should we worry about the continuing rise in this non-discretionary spending category? Do you think that if one could create some residual income that one might NOT have to worry about this item in ones' outgo? And would it make sense to believe that increases of double-digit magnitude will continue into the future? And if one does believe that, does the concept of 'residual income' make even more sense?

3. In too many, maybe all, the articles I have read about why the legacy airlines are suffering - credit is given almost exclusively to those 9-11 terrorists. While their actions no doubt have had some impact upon the airline industry, I see it more as a smoke-screen hiding the true reasons for this challenge. Just as in the early 1960's, when women started going into the work force en-mass, the true reason for their going into the work force was clouded over by organizations such as NOW (National Organization of Women) and such. The 'real reason' they were streaming into the work force was that the effect of inflation on the individual family dictated they do so - and they did - and released the economic pressure on the family unit. But, this (as far as I have seen) has never been cited as the reason for women going into the work force. Only that woman finally work up and realized that they too could CEO's, and anything else they wanted to be. In like manner, the terrorists are being used as the 'reason' for the airline chal-lenges. The truth is that economically, the legacy airlines are not able to withstand the change of the economy that is being brought about by the emerging Information Age. As I have written in the past, with the coming of this new Age, the pro-cesses of 'lifestyle creation' that were borne and worked well in the Industrial Age are now aging dinosaurs, taking their

place in history. New processes (read that: residual income) will become the process by which lifestyle WILL be created. Thus, many - if not all, of the legacy airlines, as presently constructed, will ultimately go out of business. And, the pension benefits will have to be picked up by the PBGC. This will put additional pressure on the PBGC, and on the retirees themselves. Pilots who worked their way to the top of the scale, and were promised pensions of some $100,000/year, will find themselves living on only the maximum the PBGC can pay: $44,000 and change. Heck of a hit, ain't it????

The writing is on the wall, and has been for some time. Seems that many could not read it due to the fact it seemed to also have been written with invisible ink. Now, the ink is starting to darken up, and more and more are reading the truth. Jack, the gentleman I met this morning, was saying that more and more people are starting to talk about what they need to do to take care of themselves in the future. Bernadette, his wife (who is a State employee), was saying that many, many of her State worker friends are all starting up home-businesses and such - they feel they have to! This being shared, does it make sense for each of us to work just a bit harder for our future?

Here is to hoping we see you there - Linda and I will welcome you!

Remember:

KNOWLEDGE IS POWER;
IF NOT USED, IT IS MERELY INFORMATION.

Find a MENTOR; Use a MENTOR; Become a MENTOR.

Farmer Ross

Chapter Nine: September 2004
Week Three

Gadzooks!!! Did Winter sneak in overnight while we were all sleeping?

Here it is, September, usually a nice warm month with a lot of sun, and today the sky is grey in color - and the air is very cool. Obviously, things change over time. And sometimes change comes faster than we expect. And even though we know that things (and the climate) will change, eventually, why is it that we human beings have this knack for ignoring the change we know will come - and live as if today will be just as yesterday was? I use this observation as my segue into what I found in the 'news' this past week.

1. Online real estate listings ignite fierce competition (Chicago Tribune; 09.04): The Internet promised to make house hunting easier and faster. To a large degree, that has occurred. But the power of the Internet also has helped fuel a war among brokers over control of real estate listings. And 71 percent of all home buyers use the Internet at some point in their search. Some brokers insure that their listings are seen far and wide, while others guard them like a treasure map. There are reasons for such disparities. Smaller brokers may not list their properties on their Web site, deciding that they do not wish losing a part of the commission if he allows it to be listed on another broker's Web site. "When you have the best properties listed on your Web site and nobody else does, you're going to sell a lot of property", said Steve Cook, spokesman for the National Association of Realtors. In 2003, the

NAR attempted to impose some order on its member's online listings. Obviously, the established industry wasn't enamored of those new firms, and that was putting it mildly. Recently some of the heavyweight realtors began offering deals on warranty and financing fees to clients who agreed to keep their homes off the local MLS. In that way the realty company would be able to keep the entire sales commission (seller and buyer fees - this is my insertion).

2. Double dose of relief buoys markets (USA Today;09.17.04): Investors sent stocks higher Thursday partially out of relief that the worst of Hurricane Ivan's furor had passed but also due to pleasure that the latest economic data contained no bad news.

3. US Airways can tap U.S. Loan (Sacto Bee;09.14.04): A bankruptcy judge gave US Airways permission to tap a government loan to fund daily operations. US Airways sought to assure customers that the airline has no intention of going out of business - even as it asked to skip required payments to employee pension funds.

4. Governor Arnold vetoes bill to put a teacher representative on the PERS/STRS board - sorry, cannot find the article to cite, but want to comment on this action.

CONNECTING THE DOTS:

1. The fact that a business as large as the real estate industry is, is going through 'growing pains', is not troubling. What is going on is very similar to what probably happened to the transportation industry during the change of the last Age. Remember, the transportation industry of the 1890's and the early 1900's had several businesses tied together: those that dealt with the engines (they called them horses back then!), the 'body manufacturers (they built the buggy's!), the trans-

mission/direction-change manufacturers (that was the buggy whip builder!), the fuel providers (fortunately hay was abundant here in the USA and we did not have to go to the Middle East for that commodity!). Together, they (and some I have no doubt left out) formed the Transportation Industry. Then, Ford started his revolution. All of the 'Old Guard' , meaning the established, found themselves in a war with the future - and of course, the established lost. The established will always lose to the future, for the future is all about change; change that involves 'faster' and 'cheaper' and 'better for the masses'. You know that the established is in trouble when they have to start to 'give benefit' to the consumer in order to keep what they have. That is why they are offering the bundling of financing and warranty - to keep their business. Thus, in the long haul, the traditional broker process will find itself in a process of disintegration. The real estate agents/brokers of today are having their biggest feast, and their last. For, culminating with the Home Bubble Bust, the coming period of deflation (where home prices will continue a downhill slide), the real estate industry will find itself downsizing in numbers of agents, and the whole process of buying and selling a home will change, with the consumer the ultimate winner (well, the consumer who has residual income, that is!).

2. The insurance industry learned several years back from the last two devastating hurricanes, and will not lose as much this time. But, the biggest zinger is that the market was 'buoyed' due to the lack of 'bad news'. That would seem to infer that they did not expect any 'good news' at all; maybe the old saying of 'no news is good news' is true for the market industry? Back when I grew up we looked for 'good news' - are times so tough and changing that 'good news' is becoming as rare as the Dodo bird?

3. Have you ever heard of any business that went into business with the intention of 'going out of business'? Some-

times we get to hear some of the craziest things ever said. This article was included only to keep you up to date on the airline crisis. Now think about this: you do not plan to 'go out of business', and staying in business (long term) would require you to eventually make these pension payments, yet you do not want to make them today - just in case you are not in business tomorrow? So though one hopes for the best, they must feel that the potential for them going out of business has a probability above zero. Factor in that United just announced that they must find another one-half billion dollars that they did not already factor in, in their initial forecasts, and one gets a rather bleak outlook on the coming fortunes of some of these legacy airlines.

4. What I understand is that the basic reason Arnold vetoed this bill was that he felt the State needed a more strong representational factor on the board. And his need for this is a coming $23 Billion dollar deficit that CALPERS will soon incur. Now, I do not know as I write today if this deficit is projected over the next five, or ten, years - but it is projected. And factoring in the information that the State will borrow $1 Billion dollars in order to make their payment to CALPERS for this fiscal year, one might sense a coming major challenge to this retirement fund. State employees find a great deal of solace in the mantra that 'State retirement pensions are guaranteed by law'; yet who makes these laws? And if a law can be enacted to do one thing, might not another law be enacted that affects the first law? Also, the deficit challenges that brought Arnold to the Capitol still exist, and have not been totally dealt with; yet now we hear of yet another really large (BIG???) challenge that only compounds the fiscal challenges this State faces in the very near future. Just how solid a retirement program will those currently in, and soon to come into, will exist? One might think some backup cash flow might just be a nice idea.

In 1. above I made the comment that ' the established are in trouble when they have to give benefit to the consumer in order to keep what they have'. We have witnessed this especially in the automobile industry; first lower interest rates, then money back, then a combo of the two. And why? In order to keep their business afloat - and the established is the system of dealerships around the country. With the advent of the Internet, couldn't an auto-manufacturer just have one 'rep' dealership in a given area, with the populace placing their order via the Internet and coming to the manufacturer's dealership for pickup and whatever? With a deflationary economy coming, people will not have the money to spend on cars/trucks as they do now. Yet, by eliminating a lot of cost currently associated with multiple dealerships for the same manufacturer in the same area, costs might, at best, go down - or at least stop going up. Seems like a whole lot of manufacturers who want to keep their business, realize that the old 'established' manner of doing business (all those costly middlemen!) will not work in the future, and thus, have come to realize that by 'GIVING BENEFIT TO THE CONSUMER', and tying that process into the Internet, will enable them to continue their business! That is why our business model is destined to become the BIGGEST Internet business in the whole wide world (and even the thin world too!).

A last thought popped into my head as I wrote this last paragraph: although we have a way to use our business model to purchase cars/trucks for less than the average bear out there, what would happen when one of these manufacturers changed things a little bit and we associates could get monetary benefit in making a purchase? Would it make a major difference to you whether you bought a Ford or a Chevy - if you got monetary benefit in doing so? Many times money talks louder than any commercial could ever; and ultimately we find that a 'Ford-person' or a 'Chevy-person' is one only due to indoctrination - from a father usually (that is why I did not like Fords

- he had a bad experience years earlier and told me about them continually - so of course I became a Chevy guy). Go figure how all of us come to think about different things.

Hey, have a GREAT week - maybe Summer will come back (it is raining as I write this now!), and if not, at least Fall!!!

Remember:

KNOWLEDGE IS POWER;
IF NOT USED IT IS SIMPLY INFORMATION.

Find a Mentor, Use your Mentor, Become a Mentor!!!

Farmer Ross

Chapter Nine: September 2004
Week Four

Hey! Last Sunday it was raining! Today is just a gorgeous Fall day! And I hope all of you are enjoying the day with family and friends. After church this AM, Linda and I went to breakfast with our daughter Marci - really good food, great conversation - ate on the Patio (so we got to enjoy even more the weather) - then headed home to read the paper and just relax. When you think about it - shouldn't life be more like this on a daily basis - rather than finding us on the 'mouse-wheel' - or whatever they call that round thing a mouse gets exercise on? And just how does one get to live like this daily, rather than just on a 'once-a-day-a-week basis'? Only one way I can think of: create residual income greater than your weekly/ monthly/yearly 'cost of living' is.

So, having asked this question (and knowing that many of you already know the answer), let's see what the news is telling us from the past week: (NOTE: an awful lot happened this past week, so a bit more in this issue than the norm - so my commentary will be shorter)

1. Housing prices hit milestone (Sacto Bee; 09.21.04): It took 13 years for Sacramento County's median home price to climb from $100,000 to $200,000 - a milestone reached in August 2002 - but only two more years for it to rocket to another $100,000 to a record $300,000 last month. The fuel: low mortgage rates, innovative home financing.

2. Sticker Shock (Sacto Bee; 09.22.04): The soaring cost of basic foods is giving shoppers indigestion. What is going on? Over the past several months, the cost of food for consumers has risen at a faster clip than we have seen since 1990. (Note: this is a 'front page' - 'middle of the page' - item.

3. Fed stays it course, boosts interest rate (Sacto Bee; 09.22.04): With the economy moving ahead, the Federal Reserve policy-makers boosted interest rates for the third time this year. Fed policy-makers stuck to their view that future rate increases would be gradual because inflation is expected to remain relatively low.

4. U.S. report assails Fannie Mae, cites big accounting problems (Sacto Bee; 09.23.04): Regulators have found serious accounting problems at mortgage giant Fannie Mae, calling into question it financial soundness. Regulators found Fannie Mae violated generally accepted accounting principles in its reckoning for transactions involving derivatives, financial instruments that it uses to hedge against interest rate fluctuations. Rep. Baker, R-La., called it a "sad and disturbing day for investors, home buyers and taxpayers alike....Investors have been fooled, home buyers have been cheated, and taxpayers are at risk."

5. Buyers' new car demand waning (Chicago Tribune; 09.24.04): Automakers have predicted for nearly three years that a slew of new models and an improving economy would boost sales and reduce the need for profit-draining incentives. The economy has bounced back, new models are rolling into dealerships, but sales remain relatively lackluster. Where are the buyers? Analysts contend they are staying away for several reasons: great deals led to consumers buying a new car earlier than they would have in 2001 and 2002. And people believe that housing is a better place to put money into than a car. Now, industry sales are flat, with GM and Ford saddled

with a bigger inventory of 2004 models than desired and will build fewer vehicles in the fourth quarter than a year ago. There is little pent-up demand because of the sales reaped in 2001/2002 during the recession. When consumers have less to spend, that's what slows down the market, says Jim Hall, an auto analyst. In 1985, a new car ranked third on consumers' big-ticket wish list; now it is seventh - it is no longer Ford vs... GM, it is Ford vs.. a big-screen TV!.

6. Fannie Mae repercussions (Sacto Bee; 09.25.04): The fallout from allegations of serious accounting problems at Fannie Mae has rattled investors and could bump mortgage rates down the road. Coming 15 months after an accounting scandal erupted at Freddie Mac, findings of earnings manipulation roiled Wall Street this week. The two companies, which supply trillions of dollars to the mortgage market, keep interest rates lower for home buyers. Though not guaranteed by the government, they have special privileges, making their rates lower than the norm. Alan Greenspan has warned that Fannie Mae and Freddie Mac could pose a threat to the U.S. financial system if their ability to assume new debt was not restrained. The problem is that investors widely believe that should either company get into financial trouble, the government would bail it out even though the bonds explicitly state they are not backed by the federal government. If that perception eroded, investors around the globe could become less willing to lend money cheaply and thus put upward pressure on interest rates.

CONNECTING THE DOTS:

1. Ok, 13 years to get from $100 grand to $200 - by the Rule of 72, that would indicate an inflationary rate of approximately 6%. BUT!!! It took only TWO YEARS for it to go from $200 grand to $300 grand; and by the Rule of 72, this

would indicate an inflationary rate of 36%, per year!!! Now, on to item 2.

2. Two comments here. 1) The article goes on to state food has risen 3.6% during the first six months of 2004, projecting to a 7.2% increase for 2004. 2) This article was on the front page.

3. One comment here. 1) This article was in the business page (the back section of the paper). Same paper, same date of issue (as item 2. above), two varying comments: inflation is really high (food item); inflation very low (business item). No wonder most people feel they do not really know what is going on; they feel one way (things getting better - they read that), yet have no idea why they feel so unsettled! (maybe all this inflationary stuff???)

4. Just as in the Freddie Mac challenge, Fannie Mae was making TOO MUCH money, and did not want investors to sense 'wild fluctuation's, and juggled the figures. Again, between Freddie and Fannie, I understand that they now hold paper to 75% of all mortgages. Scary.

5. And now I hear one manufacturer is offering zero-interest for SIX years - up from five. And, with fewer vehicles being made, will that cause auto workers to work less hours? Oh, and then what happens to their spending power?

6. Greenspan does see a major, although he would characterize it as not too possible, challenge to our financial system. Think about the economy we witness; less 'big-money' job creation, no wage increases (of any significant amount), the housing industry having followed the auto industry (make it easier and easier for consumers to buy - and knowing one day there will be very few left to buy), but all getting into major debt. Now, let's go to the question I raised in my open-

ing commentary: what can anyone do to be in 'safe financial territory'?

You are in the answer; you just have to use it. Linda and I were fortunate to go to dinner with Charlie and Christy last Friday night - and we had some great conversation. Conversation about you, and how they hope to be of benefit to you in the building or YOUR business. The conversation was not about them; rather about you (and us too!)   Someone old and dead - from decades ago, if not centuries, said something to the effect that ' there is no thing good or bad, it is just as you see it'. So, the financial changes and challenges that I see coming in the coming days are neither 'good' nor 'bad'. They just 'are', and 'will be'. If you accept their possibility of them being, and you prepare in the correct manner for them, you will call them 'good' changes. Should you not prepare for them, and they come, no doubt you will call them 'bad' changes. My hope and prayer is that each of you will see them as real possibilities - prepare yourself for them - and whether they occur or not, guess what? YOU WIN!!!

Remember:

KNOWLEDGE IS POWER;
IF NOT USED IT IS MERELY INFORMATION.

Find a Mentor; Use your Mentor; Become a Mentor.

Farmer Ross

Chapter Ten: October 2004

Well gang - the first 75% of 2004 is now officially in the 'history books' of life. Hard to believe that that much of this year is gone, isn't it? And, the busiest time of the year is coming: Halloween (well, I don't think this is a really important day (night?) - but to many, it is; Thanksgiving (now this is one of the all-time great days!); and then, Christmas (maybe the most important day of any year to many). The thing is, people who are not really aware of how tough the economic times will soon become, will use these days as reasons they are 'too busy till next year' to even take a look at your business model. Your mission, should you decide to take it (HEY! Does this sound like an episode of Mission Impossible?), is to find creative ways to get your friends, family, and acquaintances to take 20 minutes or so to check out how they could change their financial future. Creative in what ways?

Well, there are many ways to get anyone to take the time to see your business model: the key is to find a key dream, want or desire - then tie your business model to this dream/want/desire. You can be funny, directive, questioning - depends upon the person and the circumstance. And it all starts with your dream/goal/desire and how bad you want to change it into your reality.

Well, the bad news is that most of 2004 is history; the good news is that the fiscal year for your business has just started. Set your goals, mentor with your Mentor - and then just go get it done!

I don't see this as any kind of segue into this weeks Money Talk - so lets just see what happened!

1. Housing market's signals mixed (Sacto Bee; 10.01.04): New home prices are soaring, but a slowdown in sales has some experts wondering about a cooling-off of the market. The median sale price rose to $443,990, 23% above the figure for a year ago.

2. PepsiCo to close 4 Frito-Lay plants (Sacto Bee; 10.01.04): PepsiCo will close four factories by the end of the year as it moves to streamline production. PepsiCo said about 530 jobs will be lost.

3. Consumer confidence falls for 2nd month in a row (USA Today; 09.29.04): Consumer confidence fell in September, raising questions about the pace of spending - and possibly the prospects for President Bush's re-election.

4. Delta slashes salaries, benefits (USA Today; 09.29.04): Struggling Delta Airlines said it will cut salaries of most employees 10% across the board in January. Annual vacations will be capped at five weeks instead of six, and employees will have to pay a bigger share of their health care costs. The airline is shouldering $21Billion in debt, and has a labor contract paying senior pilots as much as $300,000 a year.

CONNECTING THE DOTS:

1. Wow! With median income less than $40,000 a year, this would imply that the ratio of income to house price is now over 11 to 1! Oh, I know many of you are saying, "but hey Ross, most families are two-income families - thus, the ratio is really closer to 6 to 1!" And yes, that is probably true - but then that just might be the bad news also. For what happens when a job is lost? Suddenly the two-income family is now a one-income family - and if another job is finally found, no

doubt it will pay less than the job lost paid. So, income con-strictions cause financial challenges - lifestyle is changed (on the downward side), and you still have to hope that a job is found. In the end, homes going for more and more, with less and less qualifications to make this purchase - portend a bad end. For those of you that remember 1991, housing ratios were in the 10 and 11 to 1 area - and two-family incomes were the norm then too. Also, earlier this week on Good Morning America, the resident economic advisor to the show was asked the question, " is there a housing bubble burst coming?" She said all the parameters (my word, not hers - but that is what she meant) were in place and showed one IS coming. She guessed somewhere in the next 12 - 18 months. Now, across America, the mind set is in place that a bust is coming - and that might be just one more part of the fuel that will create it!

2. Ho-hum. Another company closes some of its plants in order to get more productivity out of it (that is read: make more money!). Nothing new - and it will continue to hap-pen.

3. Not being political, but most everyone knows that a President cannot 'lose or make jobs' during their short time in office (whether it is four or eight years)! The creation of jobs, and the loosing of jobs, is a function of the market place - the market place of the Age. Yes, Presidents can implement pro-grams that can over time create jobs (think of the CCC back during the Depression days) - but government made jobs are just another form of corporate welfare. I am not talking about jobs that a governmental agency has to do for the public - I mean jobs created just to create jobs for people. We are in the Information Age, where we will witness the continuing loss of jobs that have existed for years; yet the creation of jobs that never existed ten years ago. Witness all those out there mak-ing money on E-Bay - just moving 'stuff', and making money. Those type of jobs did not exist until the advent of the Inter-

net. Witness more of us using our business model to create income - and you will witness MORE AND MORE people becoming more and more SUCCESSFULL. Hey, maybe you might be one of them!

4. Just an update on an airline that is facing major challenges. The sad thing is that so many good people will find the future they thought they had a few short years ago, turning into shambles. Anyone who thinks that 'their job is guaranteed', or could not be eliminated in any way, might be a bit shortsighted. Those that feel they should create a Plan B for their future will be the ones who will weather the storms coming.

Friends - the election is mere weeks away - and in the end it will not matter who wins - Bush or Kerry. Not matter in the economic sense. Greenspan will continue to raise interest rates I believe, two or three more times, to about 2.5% or 2.75%. This will give him the ability to go down as the economy turns softer and softer. But, change is inevitable. After the election, watch for the Pension Problem to be announced! I think that this challenge will ultimately be the one that ushers in the economic downturn. Fannie Mae and Freddie Mac are in the midst of making radical changes in how they do business - and the rates will go up a bit - though I do not think they will even get to much more than 6 or 7%. Why? People are broke! The money lenders can only come up with so many goofy lending programs - such as interest only payments. Hey, ultimately a 'home buyer' will find themselves 'renters' for most of their lives! And they will not find any equity in what they pay for - for people will have less and less ability to make payments with. And factor in continuing job losses. A 'Perfect Storm'?

But, you who read this have the capacity to escape the challenges that will soon come to light!   Your biggest challenge is in believing that YOU CAN MAKE IT WORK FOR YOU! Well, I got news for you: IT WILL WORK FOR YOU, IF YOU WILL WORK FOR IT!!! Yes, it takes WORK! But, heck: either work hard for a short time, or work hard the rest of your life - what makes the most sense to you? Ultimately, you choose how you will live. Remember that old saying that most of us hated when we first heard it: " The way we live today is the way WE WANTED TO LIVE - based upon the choices we made five years ago. As that old Knight from the movie Indiana Jones and the Last Crusade said: "Choose well!"

Remember:

KNOWLEDGE IS POWER;
IF NOT USED IT IS JUST INFORMATION.

Find a Mentor, Use your Mentor, Become a Mentor!

Farmer Ross

Chapter Ten: October 2004

Week Two

Tired Greetings from one who just got back from the Seminar!!! I don't mean my 'greeting' is tired - I mean I am! And, it was ALL my own fault too!!! This Seminar was just totally outstanding - and I found that this year I had different reasons for going then any of the past ones I have attended. And, one of them was to listen to the words of Jody Victor - and of Kathy, his wife too. Friday night, they both shared with all of us; then, they talked to a smaller group of us who had qualified to hear some 'special' thoughts and info. Then, this group was made smaller though the process of having to have met yet more qualifications. Then, this group was sheared a bit more by a last set of qualifications. Now, this might sound not fair - but as you know, life is not fair either. It had been announced that this would occur - and Linda and I did what it took to insure we made the 'final cut' - if you will. Was it worth it? Well, you had to be there to answer that; but for Lin and myself - YES, YES, YES!!! And at the upcoming Seminar in January next (which will be held in San Francisco!!!), there well might be another set of 'qualifications' to hear a special speaker. Those that wish to learn and cull more out of these four special convocations each year must do more. In the end, it is ALL up to each of us. We make the choice of how we will live in the 'tomorrows' by the decisions we make in the today's!

CHOOSE WELL!!!

And with that, let me use those thoughts as a segue into this week's news:

1. Gushing oil prices pound airline stocks (USA Today;10.08.04): The price of oil surged Thursday above $53 a barrel, and increasing the sense of doom in the beleaguered industry. Smith Barney analyst Dan McKenzie told clients that a proposed deal between pilots and management at Delta Air Lines won't be enough to keep them out of bankruptcy.

2. US Airways: workers should not count on pension (USA Today;10.08.04): US Airways lawyers told a federal bankruptcy judge that the carrier can't afford to maintain its current pension plans.

3. If America is Richer, Why are its families so much less secure? (L.A. Times; 10.10.04): for 25 years, government and business have forced workers to take on mounting risk. An analysis by the Times shows ever-larger swings in household incomes.

CONNECTING THE DOTS:

1. What can one say? A major 'hurt' is coming to many who have put their entire lives into one job. Retirement? At what level will any of them live?

2. More of the same. Change is coming. Get ready for a tougher day than before.

3. Because they are less secure? The Times wrote a 4-page - four FULL PAGES - for this article - way too big for me to even try to encapsulate. In essence, the fact is that workers are finding out there is NO secure, long-term job any longer! In fact, during the 1980's a business research group found that 56% of major corporations agreed that "employees who are loyal to the company and further its goals deserve an as-

surance of continued employment." Ten years later, just 6% agreed! That means that some 94% of companies DO NOT AGREE!!! That implies that they assume NO LOYALTY to their loyal employees!!! ....

I have come home, tired - but not so much physically tired, as tired of not seeing enough of you out there doing what you should be doing; and doing for you and your families. Now, Money Talk is sent to many outside of our personal group - so I am not just talking to those that are a part of this group - I am talking to anyone that is reading this. My rationale for writing this 'series' - or whatever it is - was to help keep all of you more up-to-date with what is happening in the business world - to enable you to talk with prospects (or suspects) - or even just friends and family - in a way that would indicate you are a business person; for you know what is going on in the business world. But, between this last Seminar and this last article - I feel (care!) so much more.

After the Seminar concluded Saturday night, Bill, Easy, Alex, Guy, Roger and I talked from about midnight until 2 plus in the morning - about what was said, what we needed to do, what we felt for and about each other. I went to bed not one bit tired - rather - intoxicated with the knowledge of what I was a part of and who I was associated with, and where we are going. My Friends, on a scale of 1 to 10, I - and you - are with a group that measures at least 100! Totally off the scale!!! But, at the same time - I am afraid too many of you do not feel a sense of urgency to get your business built, let alone started. Why would I feel that way? How about when I look around the room and see too few of you that I do know by name? And by dream or goal? And I can speak for Charlie and Christy, Bill and Tracey, Dave and Karen - and know they feel the same. Real change, change most still refuse to believe is coming, IS coming! The good news is that there is a 'shot' available for inoculation (unlike for the flu we keep reading about!) that can prevent 'flatdogbrokeitis' - and it is in YOUR hands. As the old saying goes, "that is both the good and the bad news". I have never before tried to push you to read any article I have reported on - but I hope, with all I can hope with, that you will go to the Internet, the library - where ever you have to go - and read this article in the L.A. Times - all four pages of it. What you will read is just the tip of the iceberg. If it moves you, then you know what you have to do. And I will know in three months when we next get to 'convocate'.

One thing I concluded from my night talk with my buddies: success in building this business has absolutely NOTHING to do with money! Not the cost for a ticket - the cost to get there - the cost to stay there - the cost to eat there - the cost of anything - for money is only a concept. What success DOES have to do with is one thing, and one thing only:

YOUR MIND SET!!!

If anyone who has read this feels I have said (written?) anything that is hurtful, then please find it in your heart to forgive me. My intention is not to hurt; rather to encourage, and with a sense of urgency. For we live in a time where change will come more quickly than at any other time in history. Those that prepare for it will get through more easily and find more success. Those that do not will suffer. Read that article, find your truths in it, and set your sail for success.

Remember:

KNOWLEDGE IS POWER;
IF NOT USED IT IS MERELY INFORMATION.

Find a Mentor, Use your Mentor, Become a Mentor.

Farmer Ross

Chapter Ten: October 2004

Week Three

Wow!

Was this a change of weather or what? All of a sudden one might think they had overslept and Winter had descended upon them. A bit on the cold side (for some) and rainy. Yup, definitely a shade of Winter.

The business news of this past week has not, for some reason, 'moved' me in the sense of wishing to report on - thus I find myself going in a bit of a different direction. Some days cause me to ruminate more than others, on what I am doing, what we collectively are attempting to do, and what it all means. Thus:

As I review this weekends activities for Lin and myself, I found it a microcosm of what life can be like when one builds one's business to a point of financial freedom. Yesterday, Lin and I - and my son and daughter (Darin and Marci) - worked on the East Wind Youth Center from 8:00AM until about 5:30PM, with about 60 other people from our church - in what I guess one could call a 'Makeover'. Emptied the entire building, painted all of the insides, repaired bathrooms, laid carpet, installed cabinets, brand new lawn out front - just made it like new! The first half of the microcosm: serving others. Can you imagine how many out there are waiting to be helped (served)? Served in so many ways. And would it not be true that the ability to serve others is to not be in need yourself? And in being financially free, by definition you would not be in need. I think Julio Melara, that fantastic speaker we heard several years ago, shared with us that too many out there have their napkin under their chin (saying: serve me) rather than stuck in their belt line (say: let me serve you).

Today, Lin and I went up to Apple Hill with Darin and Melissa (wife - and soon-to-be mother!) and thought the rain would keep the crowds small. Well, it kept some who might have been thinking of going, from going - but there was still a goodly number of folk up there. Lin and I have been doing this annually, for over 35 years - so guess it must be a family tradition by now. Anyway, probably none of this is really germane to my thought - then again it might be. My thought was this: wouldn't it be nice to have friends/family free enough to do this type of activity on the 'spur-of-the-moment'? You know, just be with people you love to be with, someone comes up with an idea of going someplace for a few days (or weeks!), and off you go! FREE! No job to worry about, no employee/s to worry about. Just FREE!!! To enjoy life as it is given to us, the beauty of the world to see and hear, and others to do it with to multiply the factor of enjoyment. Gads - isn't that the way to live? The second half of the microcosm: enjoying life with others.

Do you realize that this is what life should be? In service to others, for in serving others first, we ultimately become served. As the farmer plants his seeds, cultivates, waters - serves, if you will - upon the harvest he himself becomes served. But: first he had to serve. As a 'farmer' of this tribe, we are taught how to serve others; in word and action. The better the farmer we become, the larger the crop we can raise. And as a farmer must have faith that if he plants well, cultivates well, 'serves' well, his crop WILL COME IN. So to we must have faith in what we say and what we do. And we need to continue to learn to do it better (ah....maybe a good reason for continuing education?) so that we may ultimately serve more. Now you know more of what moves Lin and me.

CONNECTING THE DOTS:

No dots up there to be connected.........or are there?

One set of 'dots' I would like you to make a connection to deals with the following:

You have read many of my thoughts on the coming change in the economy that I sense - and my reasoning behind that feeling. The economy (I know) will change due to a number of factors: pension challenges, building boom bust, a deflationary economy. What will precipitate it? Is it possible that the energy challenge (spell that the cost of oil) will? Or, as happened after the 1990 election (when the Savings and Loan challenge was finally publicly noted by Congress) will the challenge facing the PBGC be the first domino to topple?

Your mission, should you decide to accept it, is to send me YOUR thoughts. Remember, your thoughts represent the world as you see it: thus, it has validity. Whether or not it coincides with anyone else's thoughts is not relevant. But, what I wish, and most desperately need, is to have you send me YOUR thoughts. At some time each of us has to 'connect the dots' of our truths - and when you talk to people about our business model and how it can help them - if they ask why you do it, would you best serve them by having an answer? Maybe something they had not yet thought about? So, I look forward to reading your thoughts.

Remember:

KNOWLEDGE IS POWER;
IF NOT USED, MERELY INFORMATION.

Find a Mentor; Use a Mentor; Become a Mentor

Farmer Ross

Chapter Ten: October 2004
Week Four

A Happy 24th of October to all of you!

Linda and I are still 'reeling' from the 'party' that Charlie and Christy put on last night up at their 'digs' - the Hunt Hotel - er.....Big House. I guess I was thinking in terms of 'hotel' inasmuch as they had a guest of some stature with them over the past couple of days - Lief Johnson......whooooops......as he 'really' likes to be called: DOCTOR Leif Johnson! Most of you were aware that Charlie and Christy had a 'Nuts n' Bolts' yesterday afternoon, followed by their catered dinner for those that qualified for their incentive. At the Nuts/Bolts, they rolled out a new web site they have put much time and effort into building to further make the building of YOUR business, a little easier. The launch of their business web site is official. It is not completely all 'there' yet - but much is. This happening is yet one more point that illustrates the commitment, and foreseeing, that Charlie and Christy have for all of us. Following the Nuts/Bolts, the few (and this should NOT be the case for the next incentive!) that qualified then had a most enjoyable dinner - followed by intimate conversation with Leif. Now, Linda and I will tell you that much of what was shared will NEVER be heard on any CD - not that it was 'secretive' in any way; just more personal, and .....well, the kind of talk one has with a close friend. Those that were there gained an insight into what was, what is, and what is coming, as Leif sees it. And you know what? Leif is no different than you or I. Just that he had a 'focus', and for a short time stayed 'focused', and you now know the results: financial freedom. All in all, a really great evening - and one you need to make a commitment to attend the next time it is offered. The commitment you make is not to your upline - it has to be to yourself. For why do you build (attempt?) to build your business? Oh, guess I already gave away the answer: because you are doing what you do "for yourself". Now, using this as a segue into this weeks Money Talk:

1. US Airways to cut worker pay by 21% (USA Today;10.18.04): US Airways will cut contract employees' wages 21% for four months, freeing cash the airline says it need to survive winter. A bankruptcy judge also granted the airlines request to temporarily suspend matching contributions to its 401(k) program and reduce contributions to pension plans. Its' pilots are voting on a tentative agreement worth $300 million a year (I believe it did pass later after the printing of this article - Ross) in savings. For Barry Hamel, who works at the Charlotte hub, the 21% reduction means he will make about $13 an hour; who now is cutting lawns to make up the difference.

2. Household debt a worry? (Sacto Bee; 10.20.04): The record level of debt being carried by American households and soaring home prices do not appear to represent serious threats to the U.S. economy, Fed. Reserve Chairman Greenspan said Tuesday. He said high levels of personal bankruptcies were a concern because they indicated "pockets of distress" among American households. BUT (capitals are mine!), he said the vast majority of U.S. consumers "appear able to calibrate their borrowing and spending to minimize financial difficulties."

3. An Ad found in the Parade section of this Sundays Bee: Rewarding yourself just got easier. Earn cash back with every purchase.

CONNECTING THE DOTS:

1. Put yourself in the position of any of the workers of US Airways. How would loosing 21% of your pay, today, for even just four months, affect you? Just a small difficulty? Oh heck, of course! You have at least one or two months pay sitting is some savings account, don't you? And of course, if they say just four months, that is all they mean, right? No way they could extend it to six, or eight months - or heck - why not until they find out if they really have to file BK. I am not trying to sound, or be, sarcastic - yet I think that is how what I just wrote will come across. But know what? I really don't care today. I have a tremendous amount of empathy for those souls - it has to be, no - IT IS so painful. I use the word empathy (which means to share another's feelings or emotions), for I know what it is like to lose 100% of one's income. Linda and have gone thru that. When I read about this happening to others, the feelings do return. And both Linda and I would not wish that on anyone, for it leaves you with the most empty feeling we have ever known. All that you believed in and put yourself into turns to.....well....zip. Yet, you have a family to take care of - people who depend upon you - and now what? What do you do now?

2. Not be be unkindly, but Alan is starting to sound like the 'What, Me Worry?' guy. He even had a magazine named after him. A free hot-chocolate to the first one who can name him and gets it back to me (I remember now - but the offer is still in place!). Methinks the "pockets of distress" lie between Canada and Mexico, and the Atlantic and Pacific Oceans - of course, I might be in error. And of course, we have been witness to the quality of "calibration" of most consumers. "Hey, the old household is now worth another $100 grand - let's just do a re-fi, and pay off the bills - and spend the rest." Of course, how many realize that in paying off that $30 grand or so with the re-fi just put that debt someplace else? It did not

really go away - you just think it did! 'Cause next year the old place will be worth another $100 grand. Ain't it nice to be wealthy????? Mo' money every year, and all we do is live in it!!! Gad-zooks - the guy writing this must be going zany!!!

3. Ah, the world of 'Benefit'. What is going to steer consumers to business places of business in the Information Age? BENEFIT!!! With this Visa, for each $100 dollars you charge, you get one point. Each point is worth $1 dollar, upon redemption. Maximum of $600 dollars a year. Not bad for just charging what you were going to charge anyway, yes? And have we witnessed a continuing change in how more and more products are being marketed? Discover Card was the first (according to my memory), Shell gas has benefit now with using their card, American Express, now Visa.....and who was the one that started all this 'benefit to the consumer' stuff anyway? Nutrilite was - back in the 40's! Guess you might say that we were the innovators, huh? Think about that for a moment: the company you are affiliated with went 'against the grain (mainstream thinking?)' - some 40 plus years ago - and now are leading the pack. This truth is a fact in business - and in life. Running with the pack is usually the wrong direction for success.

I close with reference to my writings in 1. above. Had to take a short break before finishing this, and while I was 'taking a break', thinking why I felt so compelled to write as I did. And I think it has to do with "my view of things to come." Massive change will come - and I believe it will come after the election. Not necessarily 'right after' - but during the coming six to eighteen months. I asked in a prior column what you, the reader, thought might precipitate it - and some of you are still thinking, I know. Hopefully, all of you - for I have not yet received any of your thoughts. But, when it comes, there will be many, many more than just the employees of US Airways in the same boat. All of you have in your hands a way 'out' of having to be able to empathize with any of those workers. As I said, Linda and I have been there - maybe some of you others out there too - and you DO NOT want to be there! What does it take to win? Leif said it all in one word: F-O-C-U-S. Leif said he has registered about 51 people - total. And look how he lives!!! How many would you be willing to register, work with, to live as he does? What if it took 100? 200? Does it matter? The question is: how do YOU want to live in the coming years? And, if change is inevitable, would it make sense to do the work today - and enjoy the rewards of not running with the pack? Again; your choice. The 'choice' is always yours - and you not only get to, you HAVE to live with its return. Personally, LIn and I choose to HAVE TO live as financially free people. What about you?

Remember;

KNOWLEDGE IS POWER;
IF NOT USED IT IS MERELY INFORMATION.

Find a Mentor; Use a Mentor; Become a Mentor

Farmer Ross

Chapter Ten: October 2004

Week Five

Hey!

It's Halloween!!!

The time of 'trick or treat' - so, in the hopes that you do not get 'tricked' into believing all that you read is true, let us see if there are any 'treats' in what is really being said!

1. 'Temp' workers struggle to make it (Sacto Bee;10.31.04): Former middle-class jobs are being filled at lower pay with no benefits. Phillip Hicks is among the ranks of what economists call the "contingent" work force, the vast and growing pool of workers tenuously employed in jobs that once were stable enough to support a family. In a single generation, "contingent" employment arrangements have begun to transform the world of work, not only for temp workers, but also for those in traditional jobs who are competing with a tier of employees receiving lower pay and few, if any, benefits. The rise of that work force has become another factor undermining the type of middle-wage ;jobs, paying about the national average of $17 per hour and carrying health and retirement benefits.

2. Sony boutiques in upscale malls irk some electronic retailers (Sacto Bee; 10.31.04): Few people took notice when Sony Electronics opened a tiny storefront last year in a swanky mall south of Los Angeles. As it turns out, the small store would represent a big change in how Sonby sells its televisions, DVD players and other gear. Some retailers that sell

Sony products worry they will lose sales. Tom Campbell, V.P. of Ken Cranes Home Electronics Inc, is watching very closely how they do. "The manufacturer is becoming a potential competitor." Abt Electronics, in the Chicago area, isn't hiding its displeasure. "We want our vendor to be a vendor, not a retail competitor."

3. No Way to Switch Off Energy Woes (Wall Street Journal Sunday; 10.31.04): Energy problems have been straining the U.S. economy and draining consumers' bank accounts.

CONNECTING THE DOTS:

1. Nope; this sure ain't what you would call a 'treat'! What it is, is just the beginning of a massive change in employment practices that cannot be 'turned off'. I understand that the Temp Agency is now one of, if not the biggest, employer in the U.S. today. And, you can see why it might be attractive to new-to-the-work-force people: temp agencies, more aptly the companies that hire the temps, seemingly pay more per hour than a 'regular' job pays. Of course, since they are new to the work force (and thus probably younger), they are not too worried about retirement processes. Heck, we know this is true of people in their forties - since so few have actually done any retirement planning during the first twenty years of working. And health benefits - well, some in their early twenty's might seek it - or want it - but for the most part they still feel invincible to the ravages of time and/or work - and so if they do not get it; 'oh -well'. In the final analysis, as more and more firms use 'temps', other firms will have to adopt the same policy to stay competitive - meaning the 'temp' will become more and more of the work force. Also, inasmuch as we are in the time of fast change, having 'temps' allows firms to become faster acting, or reacting, in these days of quick change.

2. Now why in the world would a manufacturer go to the expense of opening a brick-and-mortar store, replete with employees and overhead, when they have retailers that have already done so? Might it be the issue of 'profit'? Maybe, due to the consequence of the traditional distribution system, the manufacturer is not making what they feel is 'enough' profit. So, the thinking might go, "...if we sell directly to the consumer, could we sell it for a bit less and make a bit more?" Now, talk about Einsteinian analysis - this CEO should go to the head-of-the-class, wouldn't you think? Yes! Shorten the distribution cycle - make more money - and keep all the stockholders happy! A CEO might even think about getting a raise (or just keeping his/her job, maybe) for being this smart. But, if eliminating the distribution system, and offering a manufacturer-to-consumer process, might this CEO then come to the realization that if the brick-and-mortar and employees could be eliminated, could they make even MORE money??? And maybe, paying someone to direct traffic to their 'outlet', would be OK too; as long as they maximized their profit. Does anyone out there in reader-land have absolutely any idea of who could do this 'directing'??? In the final analysis, for any retailer out there this type of thinking (and action) definitely qualifies this to be something other than a 'treat'.

3. The continuing challenge of 'too little oil - too much demand'.   Oil in now at an almost all-time high - close to $55 dollars a barrel. Does anyone really think the cost will retreat to $40, or less? The major gas producers are announcing all time profits for the third quarter - and the Middle Eastern producers are making Billions each day. Let's see now; on the 'food chain', exactly where does the consumer fall? Oh, right there at the bottom!!! And is this challenge of higher gas prices going to cause any economic effect upon the masses? Oh yeah - going to create more and more effects - and not the good kind, either. And the oil issue is also causing major stress

on many large companies (the airline industry), and ultimately the stock market (which will affect the R.O.I. of stocks), which will affect the pension problem we face in America. No thinking has to be done on this one: this too is not a 'treat'.

So, let's now look at our bag of goodies and see how we fared: trick, tricked, and really tricked. Not one lousy 'treat' in the whole bag - why did we even bother to go out? Ah, but as one of our Master Mentor's has shared: there is nothing either good or bad, only in the way one sees it. In appearance, all we got was a bunch of 'tricks' - but, with any 'trick' - usually one can find a 'treat'. So, let's re-look at our bag of goodies: temp employment and all that comes with being a temp (low pay, long hours, no retirement), and this will be more and more the way of our world; companies finding ways to eliminate their middlemen; and the cost of energy continuing to go up, since there is a growing demand for oil, yet oil production is just about maxed out. What is left? Well, of a job does not work well any longer, and the distribution system is changing, and the cost of energy is going up, and up - what one needs is: RESIDUAL INCOME!!! If the 'temp' process is going to be king-of-the-hill, lets be a fantastic TEMP! And, why not become a TEMP someway in the new distribution system? And, due to the nature of residual income, as a TEMP, we will not put ourselves (nor or families) in a line of consequence with rising oil costs.

You notice that I refer to this TEMP as a capital letter TEMP! This is because this TEMP is smarter than the average Temp. The one place that one can become a TEMP is within our business model. For, we know from association (Frank and Barbara Morales, Jeff and Marcia Carlton, Charlie and Christy Hunt) that these guys were once TEMPS, and now have NO JOB! And, they did it using our business model. And, do you think they ever concern themselves about the cost of oil, gas - or any of their derivatives - during their days and nights? I think NOT! So, on this Halloween day/night - might it be time for one to make a decision on how one wishes to live tomorrow? The writing is on the wall - take heed.

Not that this is a religious column, but it comes to mind that somewhere in the Old Testament, one can read about a King that finds God has written some 'words' on the wall of the Kings big hall. No one can read it, but then one guy (who is on God's side) can. And he reads it to the King. And it says the King will die. But, the King does not believe him. But, the King does die. So I say: "to s/he who can read, take heed" - for the writing may not be on a wall, but it surely is out there everyday.

Remember:

KNOWLEDGE IS POWER;
IF NOT USED IT IS MERELY INFORMATION.

Find a Mentor; Use a Mentor; Become a Mentor.

Farmer Ross

Chapter Eleven: November 2004

Well, here is November - sorta snuck up on all of us, didn't it? Yup, snuck up one month at a time - as it always does. For some reason it reminds me of the old story about the frog in the sauce pan. When he got put in, the water felt just fine - what the froggie did not know is that slowly, very slowly, the heat was being turned up - bit by bit. And ol' froggie just kinda got real comfortable - water just felt fine - even though it got warmer and warmer. What froggie did not know was that there is only so much heat a frog body can take before it - well, goes into remission. Remission you say - now that is a strange way to put it. In fact, so strange that I had to look up the word to see if it fit. And you know what? It does!!! Remission is the giving up of a right. See, froggie gave up his right to life - because he did not pay attention to his surroundings. And you and me? We see the months go by, know that how we live is not how we want to live - and yet........we allow the months to go by - one by one - without putting any passion into building our business. You know, the business that would allow you to live the way you really want to live. Consider that each month we let go by is like froggie letting the water temperature go up just 1 degree. Gonna take a really long time to cook froggies' goose - but eventually, it will get cooked. How long 'till your goose gets cooked? So let's see what is driving up the temperature, let's see what life is doing to create more heat.

1. Delta offered $500 million in financing (Sacto Bee; 11.02.04): Delta got another key financial lifeline in the form of $500 million in additional financing, from General Electric and American Express. However, like the other agreements, it comes with strings - one being getting a concession from its pilots. A ratification vote began Monday, and it includes a 32.5% pay cut and other concessions.

2. United seeks to end pensions (Sacto Bee; 11.05.04): United Airlines is seeking to terminate pensions and is demanding other concessions. Facing $4.1 Billion in obligations to its existing pension plan over the next five years, United wants to terminate it pension plan and replace them with defined contributions. The government-financed Pension Benefit Guarantee Corp. would have to take on United's obligation, which has sparked worry in Washington over the potential steep cost to federal taxpayers.

3. Letter of law spelled doom of pension plan (Sacto Bee; 11.06.04): If anyone still needed evidence, United Airlines' move to terminate its $8.3 Billion pension plan shows that a company can observe federal law scrupulously year after year and still end up with a hopelessly insolvent pension fund. Of the estimated $8.3 Billon shortfall, the insurance program will cover $6.4 Billion, the work force will absorb the remainder in reduced benefits. If those companies ever tire of footing bills, they would cancel their pension plans and drop out of the system. At that point, taxpayers will have to step in.

4. Northwest pilots could take pay cuts, concessions to help ailing airline (USA Today; 11.05.04): Northwest pilots today could become the latest airline group to accept big pay cuts and concessions to help their employer survive. Northwest pilots generally rank second to Delta in pay, $273,000 a year to $320,000 for Delta. The machinists union is dead-set against concessions.

Connecting the Dots:

Let's connect all those dots above together.

Fact: The airline industry is re-inventing itself - and it has to. The old business model just will not work in the economy it has to live in. Energy is just one factor - and maybe it should be seen as just that - one factor. If we look underneath the challenge, what we might see is that one process that was created during the Industrial Age is now dying in the Information Age. Many times I have written about how my sense is that 'life style generating mechanics' created in the Industrial Age will not function as well, if at all, in this new Information Age. Many will point and say that the high cost of jet fuel is the culprit - but is it just one symptom of the disease that is truly killing the old airline industry? And let's look at the pension challenges that are now being talked about. Remember, I wrote that though these challenges were known to exist prior to the just past election, no one would talk about them - for both parties are somewhat instrumental in their existence. But now, you will see and hear about the impending disaster that awaits those that believed and trusted in the defined benefits pension plan. And, guess who will be expected to bail them out? Yes, all those people will say the government should bail them out. And if the government does bail them out, who pays for that? Oh, that's right. US!!!

Many times I have said that I feel for those that trusted their employers - to do the right thing. And most employers did try to do the right thing. Just did not work out. No one seems to look really forward to actions they take today. This has been, and sadly will always prove to be true. My question to you, the reader, is this: how far forward are you willing to look? If you are in the generation that Linda and I are in, then all of us had better get our rear-ends in gear and put together as strong a residual income as we can - or else just plan on working for many, many years - and maybe never retiring! Those of you that are a generation or so behind - get on the shoulders of us, the older generation, and get some spyglasses, and look as far forward as you can see. Massive change is coming - bet on it. And then do something about it - or relegate yourself to working till 'death do us part'. By that I mean parting from your job.

If the tone of my 'talks' seems to be getting harsher than months ago, I believe it is so. For I write not just to you - I write to myself also. And sometimes I just need a good kick in the old rear-end to make me go faster. So please be advised that I am not a 'preacher' - not only will I ' write about the walk', I will ' walk the talk'.

Remember:

KNOWLEDGE IS POWER;
IF NOT USED IT IS MERELY INFORMATION.

Find a Mentor; Use a Mentor; Become a Mentor

Farmer Ross

Chapter Eleven: November 2004
Week Two

Hello to all of you in reader-land!

Linda and I had a great time yesterday at the Holiday Extravaganza. And my good friend Bob Brown (whose wife Mary sings at our opening, songs at an altitude not yet measured on most scales - soooo gooood!), passed some information on to me that has given me 'food for thought' - and no doubt will come out in my 'Dot Connecting'. One thing that I appreciate so much is the commentary that several of you have taken time to send to me - especially in how you have used pieces of it in the sharing of your business model. Sometimes I am not sure that it is being read by many - but that is my challenge - for as I have shared several times, I write only to stimulate thought so that any reader can more deeply understand his or her 'truths' about what is happening to our economy. And having said that, I find that is my segue into this weeks edition of Money Talk.

1. Delta Airline Pilots to Vote on Pay Cut (CNN/Money; 11.11.04); Delta Air Lines' pilots union said early Thursday it had reached a tentative agreement with the airline to cut flight crew wages by nearly a third, saving the airline about $1 billion annually and giving it a chance to stay out of bankruptcy court.

The Air Line Pilots Association (ALPA) said the deal, which still needs approval from the union's rank-and-file members, was reached Wednesday afternoon. It includes a

32.5 percent pay cut, effective Dec. 1, followed by a five-year wage freeze.

The union also said the deal gives pilots the option to purchase a 15 percent stake in the airline. The package includes changes in work rules that the union said is better for pilots than other concession deals in the industry, even though they are worse than specified in the current contract.

CONNECTING THE DOTS:

1. This I call the 'first-shoe-dropping' in the changing of our economy. And I am not seeing a quadruped (four feet), but more on the order of a centipede (think that critter has about 10 legs - and thus ten shoes! - now that I think about it, a centipede might just have 100 legs - but I don't think we will hear that many shoes dropping over the coming months). Think about it; the most senior pilots make on the order of $320,000 a year. They are now taking a 32.5% pay cut - which means they will now only make some $216,000 a year (gonna be tough to live on only $18,000 a month) which would translate to a take-home pay of roughly $12,000 - or $3,000 a week. No, not trying to be facetious - just to show what they really make - and for only working maybe a third of each month (flying rules set up by the FAA as to how many hours a pilot can fly). But, the worse news is that they are also accepting a wage freeze for the next five (5) years! Now, with inflation at a nice steady 6% per year, that would mean an income of some $158,523 a year - or $13,210 a month. Still more than enough for any of us to live on - but then what? Do they hope for some type of miraculous turn-around in the economy? The airlines of the near future will look, business-model wise, more like SouthWest than Delta (as it was just last month). Pilots will continue to make less money. Factor in that United has announced that it is going to eliminate paying into their 'defined benefit pension plan' and paying

only into a 'defined contribution plan', you can see what Delta will have to do also. What this means is that eventually all of the airlines will no longer have a 'defined benefit retirement plan' they will pay into - rather, they will have only 'defined contribution plans'. This means the individual has to make their own decisions on how to invest for their retirement. And what will they invest in? Into the stock market I would imagine, but at the 'retail level' - not at the wholesale level where the real return on investment is made. And as the market continues to yield smaller and smaller dividends, and/or does not increase in value by at least 6% a year, then the retirement plan of any individual will be worth less than it was earlier. So, how will they ever retire? And, since all of the airlines are not 100% current on monies needed to fund those that have, and will, retire - who picks up the tab? You already know the answer: the Pension Benefit Guarantee Corporation (read that the U.S. Government - which means - YOU!)

As the days continue to unfold, watch and witness the continuing deluge of statements made by congressmen/women about how this challenge is growing by the day. Then, watch as they (via the media) try to find culprits - and they will name many - but they will never name themselves! And yet they are the ones that created this situation - they made the rules, and then changed them. No, this is not a one political party' mess - they are all in on it. And no, it was not something they wanted to bring about - rather something they brought about by not looking to the future and seeing what their present-day actions might bring about.

Is the pension challenge the first domino to fall? I do not know - what do you think? That I would love to read. Factor into your thoughts the challenge of energy, minimizing of R.O.I. from the stock market, wage stagnation, and rising interest rates. Most of what I listed are factors found in a Deflationary Economy. What can one do to be less harmed by this type of economy, if it does in fact come to fruition? If you would invest; invest in what? And why?

Change is coming faster than most of hope to see. We are leaving the Industrial Age - and are more fully into the Information Age than ever. If money is to be made on the transfer of information, how can one get involved in this transfer process? And if one believes, or better yet - KNOWS, that money is to be made in this medium, would it make more sense to get started now - or wait until later? Choice. It is up to each of us to make a 'choice' - and remember; if you choose NOT to make a choice, then know that you HAVE made a choice. As the old Knight in that Indiana Jones movie said: "Choose wisely!"

Remember;

KNOWLEDGE IS POWER;
IF NOT USED IT IS MERELY INFORMATION.

Find a Mentor; Use a Mentor; Become a Mentor.

Farmer Ross

Chapter Eleven: November 2004
Week Three

'To thine own self, be true.'

I believe that the Bard made this statement - you know, he is one of those 'Dogs' - Dead Ol' Guys - and the Bard was really known as Shakespeare.

This might seem to be a loony way to start a financial thought - and it probably is - but I find it a great way to share a thought or two on another subject that is just as germane to our endeavors. As many of you know, I am a musician of some report: some report I am not halfway bad; others that I may not be even that good! Nonetheless, I still play with our church orchestra and do my best. (OK, you don't have to get on your Sunday 'go-to-meeting duds - this is not a church service!) But it came to me that I should share just a short bit of what it is that creates my 'world' - if you will. What I have found is that what one declares to be their 'truth' is most often based upon what they believe - their core beliefs, if you will. One belief, that is always in my mind when I write Money Talk is the following: ' Do nothing out of selfish ambition or vain conceit, but in humility consider others better than yourselves. Each of you should look not only to your own interests, but also to the interests of others.' The first sentence has been paraphrased by none other than Dale Carnegie in his How To Win Friends and Influence People. And we all know that Dale (we are now on a first-name basis!) was the ultimate Master of what it took to make friends and influence people, don't we? The second sentence reflects one of the core values of our business model. And I find that it those two sentences are a core value of myself, and are reflected in my writings. And they form one of my 'truths' - and is found in the book of Philippians, Chapter Two, verse 3 & 4. There is one other verse that is found in another book (within the Book) also, and it says: '...a measure of wheat will cost a days wages.' And I too know that is one of my 'truths'. Thus, if you did not know what constitutes a part of my foundation of thought, now you do. And I share this information not in a 'missionary' way - but in a way for you, the reader, to start to understand why I write what I do.

The Chinese wrote, several thousand years ago, that the Ocean stays below the rivers and tributaries in order for them to pay tribute to it. Sounds crazy, maybe even stupid (I thought that statement was totally a nut-statement for years!) until one day it came upon me that it was talking about people - and not describing a part of our world. If you really want to have another hear what you have to say, then speak as though the one you are talking to has more import than yourself - and your message WILL be heard! For do you like it when people talk 'down' to you - as though they were your superior in some way? Of do you like it when they talk to you in a manner that would indicate you know more than they? The question I would ask is this: Do you want to just sound smart, or would you rather have the one you are talking to hear what you have to say? Your answer might yield some light on whether your business is growing - or dying. And if you look to the interests of others first in the building of your business, will you not ultimately strengthen your own interests? Again, maybe some insight into why your business may not be prospering as you wish it to.

That other 'truth' that is found in my Book, is found in Mathew. For years, maybe decades, I thought that the only way a loaf of bread (sometimes used as equality for a 'measure of wheat') could cost a day's wages, was to see a period of hyper-inflation. Nowadays I do not believe that will be the case. For a deflationary economy would create the same situation. And since that phrase, ' ...cost a days wages' is found in a Book that I hold to be truth incarnate, I know it will happen. And thus, now you know one more reason why I write what I say is coming. And this is a pretty good segue into this weeks report.

1. Shortfall grows at pension agency (Sacto Bee; 11.16.0): The agency that protects the pensions of more than 44 million Americans said its fiscal 2004 deficit leaded to $23.3 billion, more than doubling last years record-shattering $11.2 billion shortfall. The Pension Benefit Guarantee Corp. said that it had just $39 billion in assets to cover $62.3 billion in obligations to retirees.

2. Suppliers fear they'll be facing another Wal-Mart situation (Dow Jones Newswires; 11.18.04): Wal-Mart is referred to as the 800-pound gorilla, meaning what the retailer wants, it usually gets. Now, many manufacturers are wondering if the Kmart acquisition of Sears, making it the third largest retailer in the country, will create a second behemoth that demands lower prices. To retain their business, many manufacturers could be forced to go overseas to make products at a profit.

3. US Airways asked a bankruptcy judge to cancel labor contracts with three of it unions and to impose lower pay so it can move ahead with a plan to cut costs, reposition itself and avoid bankruptcy (Sacto Bee; 11.13.04)

CONNECTING THE DOTS:

1. This will be a continuing saga - and the story line will only get worse and worse. One or two of the legacy airlines

has made comment that they will, if they have not already done so, quit putting money into their 'defined pension plans'. This means that ultimately those that have worked for years, decades, or their entire working life, will not be receiving the pension that they thought they would be receiving. Those retired pilots that have been receiving their $100 grand a year will not see it in the near future - maybe at best some $44,000 or so a year. And those that would have received less will receive even less. And, what then of the question of who will fund this burgeoning deficit that the PBGC is generating? So many people living on so much less that what they thought they would have coming in. Might this be one parameter of a deflationary economy?

2. Well, the jungle just got more crowded - for the time being. Maybe there will be two 800-pound gorillas - for a time. What I ultimately see is that in the end, neither Sears nor Kmart will be around. For both serviced the middle-class income group - and we all know that group is in the process of disappearing. So, who will they ultimately service, if there is no one in that group to service? Yet, the question facing all their suppliers is the same one they face with Wal-Mart - can we supply what they want, at the price THEY want to pay? And if they have to go overseas to do it, do you think they will go? The economic playing field is being leveled - at the expense of the American worker - and he/she can do absolutely nothing about it. Think not? Ask the airline pilots that just took a 32.5% pay cut, and a wage freeze! Not only can it happen - it WILL!!!

3. Does anyone out there think the judge will refuse? Better for the many to have a job, than no job at all. What sad thinking - but what else will any judge think? What would you do if you were the judge? Not that you want to see a worker have to work for less - but is something better than nothing? And behind the scenes, is it possible that a judge

might receive some counseling from a higher up setting the stage for his answer to the request before him? I don't know - but I bet he gives the company what it wants. (Making a note to myself: don't look for any jobs as a bankruptcy judge!)

Well, not a great week for the average worker, huh? Or the average retiree. I have to ask you: do you want to be the 'average worker/retiree'? There are some who cannot believe that things will change as fast as they seem to be changing. So, consider the past 100 years. Business seems to change at the pace that information can be passed and/or acted upon. Back in the 1800's, early 1900's, information moved slowly (only had papers - that got their info from dispatches that came by pony express and the train - then the telegram). So, business changed slowly. Today, information moves as the speed of light - and thus change will happen just as fast. We do indeed live in a 'global village'. Whatever happens in any corner of the world we know of within 30 minutes. And, usually we see it too. Thus, be ready for a quickly changing society. Position yourself to the new economy - as you believe it will be. But: find your truth - and then act upon it. Finding your 'truth' requires a bit, nay - a lot of work. But are you worth it? Choice.

Remember:

KNOWLEDGE IS POWER;
IF NOT USED IT IS MERELY INFORMATION.

Find a Mentor; Use a Mentor; Become a Mentor.

Farmer Ross

Chapter Eleven: November 2004
Week Four

"If I speak, but without love, than I am no more than a clanging bell"

I start this issue with the above verse to further help you to understand the basis of how I write Money Talk. How ...... not why. For all I have ever written has come from my 'heart-of-hearts'. All the thoughts that I have given life to represent my mindset of what the changes we read and hear about truly infer for each of us. And these thoughts are shared with love - love of my fellow man. The 'why' is second most important. For much of what I have forecast, or described as 'what I see coming', may have caused some pain to some of you. For you understood it so differently. Yet, if what I shared was with 'love' (Agape love), then would it not make it easier for you to not be hurt? And again, I have not written as a 'forecast of what is guaranteed to occur' - only as what I see occurring. This being said, I am reminded of another verse many of you have heard and or read: There is a Season for everything.

And I believe that the Season of Money Talk is coming to its close. Change is upon us, and what I do not want is to be seen as a harbinger of bad times. Nor as a commentator sounding an " I told-you-so" attitude. These past weeks, as I poured over business happenings, I do not see 'new' stuff to comment upon - only a continuing of what I have already reported seeing. I am reminded of the Chicken Little story who told everyone he met that the 'sky is falling' - some believed, some did not. Choice. But 'choice' is best made when one seeks out facts, checks information, attempts to see if there is a logical movement afoot. For in the world of mathematics (which I love!), it is a 'truth' that ' If A implies B, and B implies C, then A implies C'. And in math, truth never changes. But, in a 'changing of the Ages', what 'was' truth in one Age does not imply it will stay a 'truth' in the next Age. This can be confirmed by each of you - if you so desire. Get a copy of The Worldly Philosophers, or find a copy, and read the first 80 pages. Then sit and think. Think about what was true in the Industrial Age, and how you might see that truth dissolving in today's business happenings. Better yet, talk to one another - share your thoughts and insight - check out what your conclusions would indicate your actions should be. The worst you can do is this: nothing.

A lot of 'nothing' is being done today, though too many do not see it as nothing. Let's see what that might be over the past week or so.

1. A new idea for California's reform minded governor (Sacto Bee; 11.28.04): If Gov. Arnold S is hoping in the coming year to fulfill his potential as a political figure willing and able to fight for difficult but necessary change in state policy, the public employee retirement system would be an excellent place to start. Pension benefits for California's public sector workers are taking an increasing share of government spending, and taxpayers remain at risk for the long-term benefits already awarded. A boost in benefits during the past several years means that most public safety employees can now retire in their 50's at nearly 100% of final salary for life, and man local workers with as much as 90% in their 60's.

2. U.S. faces trade sanctions (Sacto Bee; 11.27.04): The World Trade Organization gave the go-ahead for punitive sanctions on U.S. exports. The value of the sanctions could amount to more than $150 million a year, tiny in comparison

with the $2 billion in sanctions that the EU has threatened in its successful bid to lift tariffs on foreign steel last year.

CONNECTING THE DOTS:

1. The change proposed is what many corporations have been doing for years now: change the pension plan from a defined benefit plan to a defined contribution plan. In the first plan, retirees know exactly what amount of money they will receive for life; in the second, the retiree is the one who determines that number, based upon their investments. In the first, the retiree has no part of this decision process, just has a guaranteed number of dollars coming their way each month. And as we are seeing, defined benefit plans are going bankrupt - for they are not receiving the type of 'return on investment' that they saw during the Industrial Age. No one that I know of, or have heard of, is!!! The bad news, if California changes (and it HAS to) its plan, then the newer workers will ultimately pay the bill of not being able to retire when they want to - or maybe even retire at all. The bad news is also that for those that have, or will soon, retire, the guarantee is for a set amount of retirement income, without any guarantee of 'cost of living' increases - especially with their health plan. The cost of the health plan continues to rise, and will continue to do so. Thus, the co-pay amounts and the amount of the insurance itself will continue to rise. And, the rise will be paid for, by the retiree, out of his/her pension check. In reality, their 'take-home pay' goes down. For if the State is having trouble finding the money to continue to fund PERS (for California workers), how would the State find any more money to make COLA increases? Unless they raise the taxes of all of us. And how high can they do that and still stay in office? Remember: a retirement check is just another form of 'fixed income'. And 'fixed income' inherently implies becoming more and more broke.

2. So you thought the United States was a power unto itself? Guess again. Somehow, we got dumped into the Global Village - whether we wanted to or not. And there is probably no way this is going to change - for it is part of the change mandated by.....change. A change in the speed of information distribution; a change in the speed of material distribution; a change in the speed of the creation of information (knowledge); a change from physical boundaries to economical boundaries. Europe had, and still has, the physical boundaries of its various nations. Yet, it now is the European Union - with a common currency - and financial clout - brought about by being 'one'. Many in that community have envied the United States for years, if not decades. We, the United States, have been what most countries could only dream of being. And they could only dream of it - until now. Today, the mindset is to bring the United States down to their level. And they probably will succeed.

The question, or choice, before each of you, is this: how do you choose to live? As Kiyosaki so powerfully proves to all, each of us will live in only one of two economic lands: The Land of Too Little Money - or - The Land of Too Much Money. I challenge each of you to disprove the following statement: The processes that created wealth during the Industrial Age are faltering. If you can disprove this statement to your level of acceptance, then continue doing what has been done for the past 100 years. If you cannot, then why would you continue to do only what has been done by the masses during the past 40 years? Notice, I used the word 'only'. 'Only' would seem to imply that you would do 'more' - something that is not associated merely with Industrial Age processes available to the masses. Residual income has been available for the past 50 years, but only to some - not all. In the Information Age, it is available to all - one just needs to know with whom, and how, they wish to create it.

Be of good heart (I heard that in some movie - or read it someplace - and I like it)! Your life can be so much more tomorrow than you ever imagined. Step out in Faith and claim that which is ordained for you. "For I know the future that I have planned for you, and it is Good." God never made any junk - what He did do was to give each of us the ability to find, and work for, greatness. You just have to be willing to go 'thru the fire', become hardened and pure of mind, to reach it. YOU ARE WORTH IT. Now, go out and prove it.

In Love,

Farmer Ross

Chapter Twelve

GAD ZOOKS and JUMPIN' JEHOSAPHAT!!!

It's December!!!

One month to go and you can kiss 2004 off - it's History, Baby!!! Time indeed flies faster than we wish - and it seems that only at the end of any year do we sadly accept this truth. And then we resolve to be a bit better the next year, and then the next, and ....million things I want to share, and not enough time for a million, so let's just hit a few, ok?

Last week it seemed as I reviewed all the news, there was no news. This week: every day a new really interesting happening noted - and I could not wait for Sunday to put this baby to bed. Things last week did not move at all; this week, they are so many things happening, and happening so fast that I had better get tracking!

1. European Bank worried anew at weak dollar (Sacto Bee; 11.30.04); The euros growing strength against the U.S. dollar is "unwelcome", the European Central Bank chief said. The ECB chief also stated repeatedly that recent exchange rate developments are unwelcome, with challenges facing the countries of southeastern Europe.

2. U.A.allows more avocado imports from Mexico (Sacto Bee; 12.01.04); The Bush administration expanded imports of Hass avocados, granting the Mexican government a diplomatic victory. Consumers can expect lower prices, reflecting

the wholesale cost of U.S. produced avocados which stand at $1.08 a pound, vs. the Mexican price of $0.46 a pound.

3. Weak sales in November for top U.S. automakers (Sacto Bee; 12.02.04); The nation's two largest auto makers said they would reduce production in the first quarter of 2005 after reporting weak sales.

4. Tough times for CalSTRS (Sacto Bee; 12.03.04); With a massive funding shortfall looming, STRS began grappling with the painful task of either boosting pension contributions or slashing benefits for newly hired teachers. The funding gap is estimated to be $23.1 Billion dollars in three decades.

5. Intel to sell PC Division (Title of article in the Sacto Bee this week - I lost the issue!); Intel is placing its PC Division up for sale.

CONNECTING THE DOTS:

1. The sinking value of the dollar has just kinda come into view over the past week or two. As the dollar sinks in value, relative to the Euro and the Yen, it comes as good news for the Bush Administration, for the cost of American goods overseas goes down, and thus more of our stuff can be afforded by the Europeans. Conversely, the cost of European goods here in the U.S. goes up - and less is sold. Same challenge for Japan. The bad news is that both of those nations have a ton of U.S. Securities in their holdings, and if they decide to start to dump them (because they are becoming worth less and less), then Greenspan may be forced into raising interest rates here - thus making them worth more over there! And they hold billions and billions of dollars of our securities. And, if interest rates were to rise by one to two percentage points, what affect would that have on the construction (residential) industry? You already know if you have been reading this

column for the past several months. Rising interest rates will burst the housing bubble - but you already knew that, and I am proud of you!

2. Oh well, it is just a little fruit - hard to get too excited over hard guacamole, isn't it? Then again, might it just be the tip of the iceberg? If you are one of the avocado farmers here in California - you might be more than a little excited. Could this be another type of 'outsourcing'?

3. Now this just does not amaze me one iota. Months ago it was noted that today there are a ton of gimmicks to induce people to buy new cars and trucks, that never existed ten years ago - certainly not twenty years ago. But, to prop up sales, the manufacturers had to use 'gimmicks' to induce more sales. And maybe now people are either bought out, or realize they are more broke than they thought, or just cannot afford what they have (factor in rising gas prices). So, if they make fewer cars/trucks, then might they need fewer man/woman hours on the assembly line? And if they need fewer hours for less production, just who is it that is making less than they became accustomed to making? And could some of them have just bought that brand new, twice as big house as they had, and now the mortgage is getting a bit stiffer? Oh, better go out and find some part-time work, huh?

4. Got news for the Bee; save the headline, for one day soon they will just replace the word 'CalSTRS' with 'CalPERS'. For, if STRS is having a tougher time in getting all their investments to cover the 'nut' each year, and they no doubt invest in the same stuff PERS does, would it make sense to think PERS is having the same challenge? Yes, all the current workers have a 'guaranteed' pension dollar number - but again, this is not a guaranteed 'value' of those today dollars. When one factors in the inflation rate (oh, go re-read 1. above about possible rising interest rates), these guaranteed pension dollars shrink in value,

not number. And these public pension plans are having the same challenge that the private corporate pension plans are having. Just what is it going to take for anyone to really retire in the near future? With all that is happening in the stock market, the dollar market, the housing market, does the concept of 'residual income' start to make more sense?

5. Boy, this is a BIGGIE!!! In my world, this is to be expected. For is it not true that what Intel is getting out of might be considered a part of the Industrial Age? Manufacturing, I believe, is what the Industrial Age was all about. And what is Intel 'majoring' in now - information processing - oh, a component of the Information Age. Just one more footstep as we leave the Industrial Age behind. And while I am here, let's take a look at where all the manufacturing is being done: overseas - or someplace not named the United States of America! Sure, we still make stuff here - but watch as more and more of the manufacturing processes migrate outside of our borders - to where the cost of labor is cheaper. And if you ask any CEO, their number one job is to reduce the cost of labor. Anyway they can. And if they just happen to supply Wal-Mart, the 900 pound gorilla (yes, it gained 100 pounds over the past week!), they might have to do this price reduction process sooner than later.

Boy, all kinds of things happening out there! As this column noted months ago, there are several large dominos out there that, once one of them topple, the others will fall with it. Which one will topple first is still up to debate - don't know if there is a front-runner yet. Could it be the Pension Problem; or maybe the Housing Bubble; or can it be the rising of interest rates? We have witnessed the 'games' played by the auto manufacturers in getting buyers, until there is not much less for them to do (unless they have a 'drive it for 50,000 miles, and if you like it, then pay for it' gimmick). We have seen the real estate market 'gamed' with every kind of goofy loan, no-downs, no-principle payments, and now I find they offer a 'you tell us how much you make and we will believe you' application! No kidding!!! Just have good credit, and you name what you make (or maybe it is what you think you are worth) - and you can qualify. Now if this is not just plain stupid, then I don't know what is. And know why they do it? Because they figure that Fannie or Freddie will buy this loan too, and then the government will have to worry about how good it is. Of course, if it all falls, then you - and I mean 'you', the taxpayer, get to bail them out. By the way, do you think you might be able to work 20 hours a day, six days a week?

Started reading a book - on Goal Setting - and it is a dandy (wow - does that phrase make me old or what?). One key statement the author made I just loved: paraphrased, it means - find your truth/reality - and act on it. Time is running short - you may not believe it, but I do. Massive change will happen so fast you will not believe it could happen as fast. IF you do not do something different than what the masses are doing today, then you will get what they will get. The 'sky is not going to fall' - if it did, we would all be in the dark. But, there is a light at the end of the tunnel - you just have to get going to get to the end where the light is! You decide if the light is what you want, or if you are happy being treated like a mushroom.

Set some goals.

And then go do what it takes to hit them.

Remember:

KNOWLEDGE IS POWER;
IF NOT USED, IT IS MERELY INFORMATION.

Find a Mentor; Use a Mentor; Become a Mentor.

Farmer Ross

Chapter Twelve: December 2004
Week Two

Hey, only 12 days of shopping until Christmas!

I thought I would post that information as a service to all of you out there - knowing you are so busy, doing stuff that makes you busy. And I also think that a lot of your busy-ness is not created by your being out there in 'store-land', filling aisles, knocking over stuff pilled to the ceiling by the vendors. Know how I might know that? Heck, an article in the local rag (always wanted to use that phrase!) tells it all: 'Retail sales outlook ho-ho-hum'. And we know why too! You, having unquestionable allegiance to 'your store', are buying stuff from yourself. What a racket!!! You buy from you, and pay you. Is that really fair? More than fair - it is one of the most intelligent things any of us can do to, and for, ourselves and our family. So, what are you doing in front of your computer screen? Change what is on your screen, and go make yourself some more money!!!

Well, now that my adrenaline level is back to normal, let us just get right into this weeks edition.

1. For many investors, dollar's fall means profits (Sacto Bee; 12.11.01): Wall Street doesn't think a weak dollar is such a bad thing - at least not for now.

2. More than ever, retirement in your hands (Sacto Bee; 12.07.04): Last week's warning on the future of Social Security should have served as a wake-up call for millions of work-

ers nationwide. A top advisor to President Bush says 'there are no free lunches with S.S. In fact, there won't be any free meals of any kind in the years to come.

3. OPEC may cut oil production (Sacto Bee; 12.09.04): The possibility of a cut in OPEC production grew stronger Wednesday after the oil ministers of heavyweight Saudi Arabia indicated he was aware of majority sentiment in favor of a reduction. "Our objective is to keep the market balanced and keep it stable," Saudi Oil Minister Ali Naimi said in Cairo.

4. Higher oil prices are here to stay, federal study say (Sacto Bee; 12.10.04): While the recent flurry of record oil prices may be temporary, government analysts said that $30-a-barrel oil should be expected for decades to come.

5. Lenders tell airlines: Get your act together (Sacto Bee; 12.12.04): While the airline industry received many breaks after 9-11, the are not getting them any longer. "There is simply no patience for the industry not to fix its own house," the Chief Financial Officer of Delta Air Lines stated. Where once the idea of losing an airline was unthinkable, both the government and lenders seem perfectly willing to let that happen.

CONNECTING THE DOTS:

1. Well, to paraphrase one of my Mentors, 'there are no such things as good or bad times; it is all in how one is situated'. Yup, Kiyosaki says that (though with different words than I used). See, it all depends on what side of the coin you happen to live on. Today, if you happen to live on the European or Japanese side, the fall of the value of the dollar is 'bad news'; if you happen to live on the American side, it is 'good news'. Yet, isn't it true that however the dollar fares, in the end it is just 'news'. The deal is to make sure you were positioned such that the 'news' became YOUR 'good news'. And how

does one do that? Probably a lot of answers for that question, but in the end I believe that one has to basically understand the 'season' the market is in, and act accordingly. And understanding the 'season', especially the economic 'season' - is paramount to ones success (or failure).

2. This statement was the lead for a local financial columnist - and he is only sounding what many others have said for years. In fact, this truth has been sounded for over a decade (if not decades!); just that most people have not taken to believing it. They always felt secure with the company (whether public or private) pension plan - the ones 'guaranteed by law' especially. Now, many are finding that that security was founded more on sand than rock - that that security was in basis founded upon assumptions. Assumptions that once were a 'truth' - but were miscalculated as being unchangeable. Again, this statement of one being more in charge of ones retirement is, and will continue to be, sounded by more and more. Thus; know and understand the season you are in, and act according to the demands of that season that yield success.

3. Oh, I really like this one! 'Keep the market balanced and stable'! What this really might infer is that now that the oil producers know what $40 and $50 dollar-a-barrel tastes like, they really do not want to go back to the cheap stuff. Kinda like if you used to drink $2-buck-chuck (which I hear is not all that bad), then taste a $20 a bottle of better stuff, your taste buds vote for the $20 stuff every time. The key is to afford it. And since OPEC controls the vineyard, well, guess they want the better tasting stuff. While they may not be able to keep oil at $50, they can keep it in the $30-$40 range - and all of us out here with SUV's, and Kia's too - will just have to ante up the cash to make these 'horses' take us where we need to be taken to. Sounds like a Monopoly to me, and one might wonder if the World Trade Organization will step in and help us? (Hint: don't bet on it anytime soon!)

4. Sometimes our government acts like newspapers; they tell us what happened yesterday, forgetting that we watched or heard it happening. Yet, headline it like it is breaking news. Note the date of #3 and #4 above. And really, didn't we all know that the days of $1.50 gas is history! Heck, I remember $0.29 a gallon gas - and that is only 4 decades ago. And it had lead in it - and that was when cars were cars. Ask Dave Waddell about it - he still has one or two of the really good 'cars'! Of course, they don't run as well as they did then on today's 'lead-free' gas. Oh well, life just gets better and better.

5. And what is the major problem in running an airline today? Well, jet fuel is right there at the top of this list. And jet fuel, coming from oil, you just know that it will not be getting cheaper soon - or ever. Well, maybe I should not say 'ever'. I have learned never to say 'never' - it always seems to come back to bite you when you do. But, the gist of the challenge the airline industry has is just a pre-cursor of what will happen to more, and faster. Change.

The airline legacy carriers are all pretty much founded on the same business-model. And it worked very well for a long time. But, now we are in the Information Age, and with this change of Ages comes change. One thing that is changing is that the old business model the legacy airlines have in place no longer works. The newer business models, put in place by such as South West, do work. So, if the legacy airlines want to stay in business, they have to re-design themselves. And the workers have no choice but to get in place. Either that, or lose a job. We witness airlines personal, primarily pilots, taking massive pay cuts, and more pay cuts are in sight. They have to - or retire (if they qualify). And if they do, and the airline ultimately goes BK, then the pensions these pilots and others worked for and earned will be downsized massively.

Whew!!! Just back. You did not know that I started writing this about 12:30 (Sunday afternoon), but had to quit to go and play for the last two performances of our church Christmas presentation. It is now almost quarter to one (AM!), but during the first performance I had some really wild thoughts come to mind. And I will expand on them in soon to be written M.T.'s. But, I want to put this issue to 'bed' (as they say in newspaper parlance) and get it on the cyber waves. I will give you a hint: think about understanding what 'the season is'. Stuff that has been whirling around in my head for the past month or so came to a point of clarity for me - and that is what I find I need to share next. By understanding what 'season' one is in can give direction to what needs to be accomplished; especially to be successful.

So, 'till next time, have a GREAT WEEK!!!

Remember:

KNOWLEDGE IS POWER;
IF NOT USED IT IS MERELY INFORMATION.

Farmer Ross

Chapter Twelve: December 2004
Week Three

Christmas is around the corner, everyone is really busy.

Times may change, but the busy-ness of life does not.

Thus, this will be a quick issue.

1. "Prospects for retiree health coverage are slowly disappearing for America's workers, and retirees who have it will be paying more." Drew E. Altman, of Kaiser Family Foundation. (New York Times; 12.15.04)

CONNECTING THE DOTS:

1. Well, how does one connect just one dot? This is the future, and the future is just around the corner. Just that most people do not want to look around the corner - they would rather wait to see what does happen, rather than prepare. A lot like that critter that keeps its head in the sand. Is it possible that the thought process is something akin to ' if I don't see it maybe it won't happen?' Like sitting through a scary movie - hide your eyes and it can't happen to you.

Here is a scary question: Given that health care costs continue to go up and up, and retirees pay more for it each year, do you ever want to become a retiree? What if fewer and fewer did retire? Read an article on that premise - and the outcome is not good at all! Consider, more and more graduates, both high school and college, fewer older workers retiring. Where are all these new jobs for the incoming work force? And if more and more want to work, will the age old truth of 'supply and demand' ultimately make the pay of most jobs go DOWN? For if the supply is high, then does not the cost (demand) go down? So more and more will work for less and less? And remember, if wages do not go up, then from inflationary action, the pay actually goes down - even if the number paid does not go down.

The concept of 'Time Value of Money' will finally be taught to, and understood, by more than ever before. And life will be the teacher. Money 'spoken into existence' has no time honored value - only a time honored number assigned to it. A ten-dollar bill will always be a ten-dollar bill - yet what it buys today, it will not buy one year from now. It will buy less. Need more ten-dollar bills? Use more of your time to get them. Running out of time? Clone yourself (if it is possible or legal). Can't? Then learn to live on less. Retired and can't work any longer? Live on less. Fixed income? Learn to live on less each year. Gad zooks!!! Is there any good news out there? Yup! Create residual income. A lot of it. Then, no matter how much that ten-dollar bill will buy, you will have all the ten-dollar bills you need! Won't need to work longer; won't need to work at all, maybe! And when you do retire, you will be 'RETIRED'! Meaning, living life each day as you choose, not as life dictates you have to.

Next week is Christmas. And I won't be writing anything. So you won't be getting anything from Money Talk.

But, the next Sunday, you will.

And I believe it will be a 'barn burner'. Have your fire extinguishers at side, and maybe some Maalox for your stomach. 2005 will be a year of change most will not believe could happen - and sadly, most will not be prepared for.

If ever there was a time to prepare for the future, now is it.

Remember;

KNOWLEDGE IS POWER;
IF NOT USED, IT IS MERELY INFORMATION.

Farmer Ross

Oh, and: MERRY CHRISTMAS!!!!!

Chapter Twelve: December 2004

Week Four

Hope all of you had a wonderful and Merry Christmas.

One thought is all I would pass on for this issue.

1. CHRISTMAS.

CONNECTING THE DOTS:

1. What is 'Christmas' really all about? Many recognize Christmas as the day that one named Jesus came into this world. Though there is disagreement over who Jesus was, there is less debate about what He taught. Not only what He taught, but what He did, shared, and exemplified. SERVICE. That we all need to be of service to one another. That the highest order of life is found in being of 'service' to others. Not self-service; rather other-service. Julio Melara re-iterated that thought some years ago. We celebrate Christmas by the giving of presents to another - and then find that we also receive. And it is written that 'it is better to give than receive'; and yet one truth within our world is that 'if you help enough get what they want, then you will get what you want.' SERVICE. A farmer gives to his seeds, which become mature, and become what they were designed to be. He tends, waters, cares, and weeds. He serves. And in the end - he receives. Thus, would it make sense for you to find those that have a need, help them satisfy that need, and then find that in your service to them, your own needs are satisfied?

Know the 'season' you are living in. Those that understand the 'season' and are of 'service' will find unlimited success.

Merry Christmas!

Farmer Ross

About the Author

The author of this book is just like most every other American in this country. Graduating from high school in the 1960's, and having heard the mantra of the times from both Mom and Dad of "go to school, get a good education, go to college, get a better job, work hard and retire to the Golden Years." Funny thing happened on the way to the Golden Years – they disappeared. Ross J Stone did go on to college, receiving a Bachelors degree in Mathematics, and a Masters in Engineering. Unfortunately, between the Math degree and the Engineering degree, he found that the profession he wanted to go into, teaching high school Mathematics, was more of a baby-sitting job then he expected. Thus, his move to the Engineering degree. During this process, Ross did enter the teaching profession: teaching a Building Construction program for high school seniors in a vocational program. After five years, he left to work full-time in his construction company. After some fifteen years as a designer/builder of custom homes, he started another business. One that would ultimately cost him close to a million dollars – in losses. It is said that fire refines gold – and each of us is worth gold – though most do not believe it. I understood there had to be a reason for my fire – and I found it.

Though I spent some ten years in college, learning much – but really not much – I found myself involved with a business much different from the typical business. To better understand what I was involved in, and with, I found that I needed to – nay, had to – re-educate my mind. Fortunately I was able to stand upon the shoulders of two Giants: Larry MacCracken and Robert Kiyosaki. Much of the country has heard of Robert Kiyosaki and his books – fewer have heard of Larry MacCracken. Yet, both are Giants. Their teachings gave me the ability to think as never before. Not prior to college, not after college. Not as the masses think, but as the '2-percenters' think

The author is no one really special – well, he is to his family – but his goal is to help others find a different perspective of financial goings, what they might mean, and how to best prepare themselves and their family for the startling changes about to occur in the American economy

www.ingramcontent.com/pod-product-compliance
Lightning Source LLC
Chambersburg PA
CBHW031839170526
45157CB00001B/358